THE AMERICAN ECONOMY BETWEEN THE WORLD WARS

THE AMERICAN ECONOMY BETWEEN THE WORLD WARS

JIM POTTER

A HALSTED PRESS BOOK

JOHN WILEY & SONS
New York

First published in the United Kingdom 1974 by
The Macmillan Press Ltd

Published in the U.S.A. by Halsted Press, a Division
of John Wiley & Sons, Inc., New York

Printed in Great Britain

Library of Congress Cataloging in Publication Data
Potter, Jim.

The American economy between the World Wars.

"A Halsted Press book."
Bibliography: p.
  1.   United States—Economic conditions—1918–1945.
1.   Title.
HC106.3.P57   330.9′73′091   74–7104
ISBN 0 470–69553–6

Contents

List of Tables

Preface

THIS book was originally commissioned as one of the 'Studies in Economic History', edited by Professor M. W. Flinn on behalf of The Economic History Society. The size and range of the subject matter made it impossible to restrict the length of this survey within a volume short enough for the 'Studies'. Nevertheless the original purpose of that series has been retained in this book. It has been written as an introductory guide to a very large subject. It does not set out to be comprehensive, but is intended to provide students with a fairly simple factual outline and with suggestions of differing interpretations.

It is assumed that British readers, for whom the book is primarily written, are not familiar with many aspects of American life. Where necessary for an understanding of economic conditions, problems and events, an explanation has been given of the relevant American political institutions and historical background. Since the approach is primarily analytical, the discussion is usually topical rather than chronological; to offset the lack of a systematic narrative account, a brief 'Chronology of Events' is given at the end of the book (pp. 157–65).

The book therefore aims firstly at providing basic information about the American economy between the two World Wars and a great deal of data (not all of which is exhaustively discussed) is presented in tabular form throughout the text. Secondly, it attempts to indicate the main interpretations and controversies involved. But thirdly, in the belief that distance can sometimes provide different perspectives, the book from time to time suggests new views and approaches. Comparisons are made, for example, with contemporaneous British conditions and problems. Attention is also drawn to important demographic data which have been largely neglected in previous accounts of this period.

Despite its extended length, the book remains no more than a summary account, often of exceedingly complicated matters. Much detail has been omitted and many topics, worth a whole chapter to themselves, have had to be treated in two or three paragraphs. It is hoped that this compression has been achieved without undue simplification, but it has necessitated the omission of much which might have been deemed worthy of inclusion. The areas treated the most sketchily are generally those for which a large literature already exists : for example, the Wall Street crash, trade unions and business organisations do not receive the attention devoted to them in other works; several important New Deal innovations, such as the Tennessee Valley Authority (T.V.A.) are no more than mentioned in passing. It should also be emphasised that this book does not attempt to explore the complex problems of international banking and finance in the twenties and thirties; it is intentionally concerned almost exclusively with the American internal economy. Similarly the account deliberately stops short before the outbreak of the Second World War in Europe. If such gaps are to be regretted, the author can merely plead that considerations of length made it necessary to limit the range of the book.

Rather more emphasis has been placed on the 1920s than on the 1930s, partly because of the abundance of literature about the New Deal, partly because of the belief that an understanding of the twenties is essential to an understanding of the thirties, partly because of the prevalence of serious misinterpretations of the 1920s (revealed annually in examination scripts), but also because of the enormous intrinsic interest of that neglected and misrepresented decade.

In its manner of composition also, the book varies somewhat in its treatment of the two decades, if only in the fact that the earlier chapters have more references than the last two ! This results from the circumstance that the two chapters on the New Deal are based on a series of seminars for third-year graduate students held at the London School of Economics for several years past. These seminars have been addressed by many eminent visitors, some reflecting on their own memories of Washington D.C. in the 1930s, others (especially more recently, as the passage of time has made personal reminiscences more difficult to obtain) speaking from the viewpoint of their own academic expertise. Since the evidence is not always clearly identified, a collective acknowledgement must be given here to the contributions of this long line of guest speakers, as well as those of past and present colleagues in London : Charlotte Erickson,

R. C. Estall, W. Letwin, E. J. Mottram, R. H. Pear and L. H. Pressnell.

London School of Economics   JIM POTTER
February 1974

Introduction

THE practice of the political historian of dividing history into periods demarcated by wars or treaties is not necessarily appropriate for economic history. The first question to be asked is whether the inter-war years in America in any sense constituted a 'period' from an economic point of view. What, if any, unifying features are to be found in American economic life between 1919 and 1939? If those years cannot be regarded as one single 'period', can they be divided into sub-periods which have any greater significance?

At first sight the inter-war years in America seem to have few features of economic unity. Indeed the year 1929, the mid-point, is often regarded as one of the great divides in American history. The Wall Street crash, which occurred late in 1929, precipitated the economy into an unprecedented depression and seemed to bring to an end a century and a half of almost unbroken expansion. All the preceding setbacks, though frequent, had been relatively mild compared with the catastrophic events which were soon to follow in the early 1930s. In this view, 1929 brought an end to the general economic conditions which had prevailed in the nineteenth century. The events of that year are seen as symbolising the final closing of the American frontier, not merely in a territorial sense, but also in the imposition of a need for new attitudes, towards work, profits, even the accepted goals of economic endeavour. The year also marked the beginning of a new view of the role of the federal government in the nation's economy, or at any rate of an abandonment of the old assumptions. With the 1930s came the end of the Jeffersonian dream of an uncontrolled, agrarian America and the beginning of the Hamiltonian nightmare of a government-supervised urban society. If 1929 is regarded in this way as a historical turning-point, then the notion of a unified 'inter-war period' seems remote from reality.

This view of 1929 as a great divide has been strongly reflected in much of the writing about the inter-war years. The two decades have often been depicted as quite separate and distinct : the twenties are seen as the Age of Prosperity, the Jazz Age of wealth and hedonism; the thirties as the Age of Depression, the Blues Age of poverty and despair. The two decades are represented in quasi-Hegelian terms of thesis and antithesis, or alternatively as a demonstration of the puritanical concept of retribution, with the miseries of the thirties following inevitably as some kind of hellish punishment for the godless self-indulgence of the twenties. This is an interpretation with great appeal to guilty American consciences about wealth, and to the tradition of rural Puritanism with its 'haunting fear that someone, somewhere, may be happy'.[1]

Yet, though there is something to be said for this view of 1929 and for presenting the twenties and thirties in such stark contrast, at least as a commentary on social life, such a sharp division is not necessarily any more acceptable for purposes of economic analysis than the assumption that the First World War and the Second World War sandwiched between them a unified 'inter-war period'. Both views overstate and oversimplify the characteristics of the two decades and obscure certain underlying common features. It is therefore necessary to attempt on the one hand to identify the features common to the two decades and on the other to subdivide them still further into shorter 'periods'. With some qualifications to be made later, the simplest framework is a fivefold division of these years into the following :

1918–19	Maintenance of war economy, with continuing exports to Europe and post-war boom.
1920–1	Post-war recession and readjustment.
1922–9	Economic expansion and prosperity.
1930–3	Economic collapse and severe depression.
1934–7/9*	Economic recovery.

This survey will concentrate largely on the last three of these divisions, implicitly defining the inter-war period as starting with the upswing of 1922 and ending with the outbreak of the Second World War.

Chapter 1 deals briefly with the years down to 1921, in so far as

---

* The reason for this ambiguity of dates will be explained later. Suffice it to note at this stage that 1938 saw a very sharp setback to the economy, with recovery in 1939 to much the same level as that achieved in 1937.

these have to be regarded as setting the scene for subsequent events. Chapter 2 then goes on to examine those aspects of American economic and social life between the wars which appear to demonstrate continuity rather than contrast, or at any rate to establish preconditions which were broadly common to the two decades. The subsequent chapters give an accounut of the major sub-periods, 1922–9, 1929–33, and 1933–9. This threefold division is easily represented by means of a simple graph.

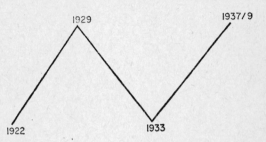

The following quantities may be added to give flesh to the above skeletal diagram.

TABLE I

Summary of economic trends, 1922–39

	1922	*1929*	*1933*	*1937*	*1939*
Number in employment (million)	40	48	39	46	45
Index of manufacturing production (1899 = 100)	194	364	197	376	374
Gross National Product (1929 $ billion*)	76	104	74	109	110
Per capita G.N.P. (1929 $)	689	857	590	846	847

SOURCE: U.S. Department of Commerce: *Historical Statistics of the United States' Colonial Times to 1957* (1960); ibid. *Statistical Abstract of the United States* (annual); ibid. *Biennial Census of Manufactures* (1921 and alternate years).

* The word 'billion' is used throughout in the American sense of one thousand millions. Thus one 'billi-buck' equals $1,000,000,000.

The diagram and Table 1 <u>both indicate that the depression of</u>

1930–3 set the economy back approximately to the point of departure of 1922, while the post-1933 recovery restored it roughly to the level of 1929.

Chapters 3 and 4 examine the features of the boom and collapse of 1922 to 1933 and discuss the economic connections between the two phenomena. Finally Chapters 5 and 6 examine the attempts of the federal government during the presidencies of F. D. Roosevelt to solve the economic and social problems of the depression, and estimate the success of those attempts.

From Tanks and Torpedoes to Tractors and Tin Lizzies 1918–21

1 POST-WAR BOOM AND RECESSION

The United States entered the First World War in April 1917 and was actively engaged until the Armistice of November 1918. Although the American economy was affected by the war in one way or another from the time of its outbreak in Europe in 1914, the main direct effects were felt in 1917 and 1918, while in many respects conditions in 1919 constituted a continuation of the war economy.

The war gave an impetus both to agricultural and industrial expansion. From 1917, with the enrolment of some 4.5 million men into the armed forces, labour shortages were felt and attention was directed particularly to improvements in productivity through intensive capital investment. In agriculture, for example, the labour force increased slightly until 1916, when the highest-ever figure for farm employment (13.6 million) was reached. (Since that peak there has been a continual, though irregular, decline to today's figure of 3.3 million.) Land was increased by 50 million new acres brought into cultivation (an increase of 5 per cent); but the greatest increase was in the value of farm machinery, which approximately doubled, from about $1.6 billion in 1913 to $3.3 billion in 1919. By November 1918 some 9 million people were working in war industries, about one-quarter of the total labour force.

The burden of America's relatively brief participation in the war was economically less severe than that of the major European belligerents. The gross cost of the war has been estimated at $177 *per capita* for Americans, compared with $525 for the British, $293 for the Germans and $280 for the French; or at 8.7 per cent of current American national wealth compared with 34.5 per cent of

British, 31.6 per cent of German and 19.4 per cent of French. Nevertheless, American governmental expenditure on the war, i.e. the excess of expenditure on the war over the probable peacetime expenditure, exceeded the total expenditure (including that on all earlier wars) of all federal governments between 1789 and 1916, approximately $30 billion compared with the previous aggregate of $27 billion. About one-third of the sum represented loans to the Allies. Total American war deaths in the First World War (killed, missing, deaths from war-attributable disease) amounted to just over 100,000, compared with German losses of 1.8 million, Russian 1.7 million, French 1.4 million and British 950,000. (American deaths attributable to the Vietnam War are estimated at about 50,000.)

During the war period American merchandise exports, especially foodstuffs, expanded rapidly, reaching a value of $8 billion in 1919 and 1920 (11 per cent of national income), about four times the 1910–14 average; the surplus of exports over imports in 1919 was $4 billion, about eight times the 1910–14 average. Moreover American ships were now carrying over 40 per cent of American foreign trade compared with 10 per cent before the war.

Revenue did not keep pace with the massive increase in Federal Government expenditure and deficits accrued of $1 billion in 1917, $9 billion in 1918 and $13 billion in 1919. The American national debt increased tenfold, to $26 billion, or 37 per cent of the annual income, estimated to have been $70.2 billion in 1919. Wartime inflation raised retail prices to a level in 1919 about 80 per cent higher than that of 1913, with average hourly earnings rising by about the same amount, but with very uneven distribution of the increases.

Even before the Armistice the call for a quick return to 'normalcy' began to be heard in America. As in Britain, the war had involved the government in the nation's economic life on an unprecedented scale. The interventions included direct controls over production, labour and foreign trade, the regulation of capital and the securities market, food rationing and a complete takeover of railways and shipping. From the Armistice and into 1919 the process of dismantling the wartime apparatus went on rapidly, but the clock could not simply be put back to 1913 : too much had changed, too many lessons had been learnt. The income-tax introduced by Woodrow Wilson in 1913, for example, became an important weapon of wartime fiscal policy and has continued, with many changes, to the present. The war led to an abandonment of the previous trust-busting policy of pre-war governments;* business agreements which had formerly been regarded as anti-social conspiracies had been transformed by the stress of war into laudable examples of patriotic co-operation, and the government actively encouraged, and in some cases enforced, such co-operation between businessmen. When the war ended, there was no return to the pre-war anti-trust crusading spirit.

The year 1919 presented the paradox of a continuation of the war economy in many respects, but its deliberate repudiation in others. The peak of the economic expansion specifically associated with military activities occurred in August 1918 and the early months of 1919 saw a brief recession with factory employment declining to about 10 per cent of the wartime peak. By April 1919 however the winter's setback was over and in the spring the pent-up demands of the war years burst through the dams. The remaining months of 1919 saw a massive, consumer-based expansion; industrial production rose by 25 per cent and retail sales still more. Exports also rose, mainly to satisfy Europe's post-war craving for goods of all kinds, but especially food. The post-war boom of 1919 also included a rapid expansion of building construction and of investment in industrial re-equipment. These processes were strongly reinforced by both the fiscal and monetary policies of the federal government. In the field of banking the newly established Federal Reserve System (set up by the Act of 1913, just before the outbreak of war in Europe) was now on trial for the first time and throughout 1919 the wartime easy supply of money was maintained.

The buoyancy of the American economy during 1919 was seen above all in its ability to absorb the increase in the labour force which resulted from the rapid release of some $2\frac{1}{2}$ million men from the armed forces, without significant unemployment. The average unemployment rate in 1919 was under 2 per cent. Yet socially and

---

* This was first embodied at federal level in the Sherman Anti-Trust Act of 1890 which President Theodore Roosevelt began to apply with some vigour in 1902. In 1914 the position was that the size of industrial corporations was considered less significant than their behaviour, with the Clayton Act of 1914 attempting to classify those types of behaviour, including such devices of collusion as price-fixing agreements, which were to be regarded as illegal. The Federal Trade Commission was set up by the Clayton Act to enforce its provisions, but for the duration of the war it was given a quite different task.

industrially 1919 was a turbulent year, with some 4 million workers at different times on strike or involved in lockouts. Race riots flared up in Washington D.C. and Chicago. The United Mine Workers, led by John L. Lewis, launched a major campaign for wage increases. A three-month steel strike at Gary, Indiana, ended in failure in January 1920.

Nevertheless the year 1920 opened in an atmosphere of optimism and prosperity, but this was short-lived and the post-war boom soon collapsed. As if to symbolise the forthcoming depression, of spirits as well as of the economy, the Volstead Act came into effect in January 1920, prohibiting the sale of alcoholic beverages. In that same month began a short, but severe, depression which eventually reached its trough in the summer of 1921. Total employment contracted; unemployment reached 1.7 million in 1920 and 5 million (over 10 per cent of the labour force) early in 1921. The recession saw wage reductions and a further continuation of strikes in industry. Domestic peace was disturbed by outbursts of activity by the Ku Klux Klan (K.K.K.) and by the anti-Red hysteria exemplified in the Sacco–Vanzetti trial.

This recession was caused above all by the ending of the post-war spending spree of domestic consumers. This was reinforced by the curtailment of government expenditure, the succession of wartime deficits being followed in 1920 and 1921 by deflationary surpluses. That the decline did not degenerate into a panic was partly due to the encouragement given by the Federal Reserve System to banks to allow advances to firms in temporary difficulties. Interest rates were raised, but there was no general curtailment of credit and the downfall was weathered without the kind of financial collapse that had in the past accompanied similar recessions.

The year and a half of economic slump was an unhappy experience. The recession, in the United States, as in Britain, brought a rude awakening from the wartime dreams of a better world of perpetual economic well-being. In September 1921, with 3½ million unemployed, President Warren Harding called a Conference on Unemployment under the chairmanship of Herbert Hoover. During the summer and autumn, however, the first signs of recovery were appearing and by the end of 1921 the American economy had turned the corner and was on the way to the massive expansion which characterised most of the next eight years.

II STRUCTURE OF THE UNITED STATES ECONOMY AFTER THE FIRST WORLD WAR

During the First World War the American population passed the one hundred million mark, and in the Census of 1920 amounted to 105.7 million. Of these, 94.8 million were white, comprising 81.1 million native-born Americans and almost 14 million foreign-born (or 13 per cent of the total population); 10.5 million (just under 10 per cent) were black native-born Americans.

In 1920 almost one-half the population (51.6 million) was still rural, living in places of below 2500 inhabitants. At the other extreme, just over 10 million lived in the three giant cities of New York City, Chicago and Philadelphia. The state of New York, with 10.4 million, had the largest population; Nevada with 77,000 had the smallest. The biggest state of today, California, was in eighth place with 3.4 million. The South accounted for just under one-third of the total population (33 million).

As noted earlier, the total number of persons engaged in agriculture (and also the total number living on farms) reached its greatest in all American history during the First World War. Although the 1920 Census was the first in the nation's history to show a fall (compared with the previous Census) in the numbers dependent on agriculture, 31.6 million people (30 per cent of the total population) still lived on farms in 1920.* The average size of American farms in 1920 was just under 150 acres. Well over three-quarters of the 6.4 million farms were 'small', i.e. between 20 and 175 acres; 12 per cent were under 20 acres, while only 3 per cent (217,000 farms) were over 500 acres. About two-thirds of all farms (4 million) were worked by the owner; 2.4 million were tenancies, including 2 million share-cropping (or other non-cash) units of which 60,000 were operated by black people. Out of a total labour force of 42 million, about 11 million gained their livelihood, either as farmers or labourers, in agriculture. As Table 2 indicates, agriculture still provided employment for more persons than did manufacturing.

---

* In 1970 out of a total population of 210 million, approximately 15 million persons were wholly dependent on agriculture, or out of a labour force of 80 million, only 4.5 million (or 5 per cent) were employed in agriculture. The apparent discrepancy between 'persons dependent' and 'persons employed' results from the generally larger size of farm families compared with urban families.

TABLE 2

Structure of employment in the United States in 1920

	Number in millions	Percentage of total
Agriculture	11.4	27
Manufacturing	11.0	26
Private services	5.0	12
Trade	4.2	10
Transport and public utilities	3.1	7
Construction	2.2	5
Government	1.9	5
Mining	1.2	3
Finance	0.9	2
Other	1.3	3
Total	42.2	100

SOURCE: Bureau of the Census, *Census* of 1920.

If these groupings are re-stated, we find that primary production (agriculture and mining) gave employment to 30.4 per cent of the labour force, secondary activities (manufacturing and construction) to 31.4 per cent, while the tertiary sector of the economy (all service functions) emerges as the largest, providing 38.2 per cent of total employment. (Comparable figures for 1930 and 1940 are given in Table 9, p. 39, where the 1920 figures are also presented in re-arranged form.)

Owing to the post-war recession, the Census of Manufactures of 1921 showed slightly fewer industrial wage-earners than in 1914, a total of almost 7 million.* Six main industries provided employment for about two-thirds of all industrial wage-earners (figures in thousands): textiles (1511); iron and steel production (1032); lumber and wood manufactures (675); food processing (569); paper and printing (467); and railroad repair shops (418). Similarly six groups provided an industrial 'value added' (the value of final product *minus* cost of raw materials) of over one billion dollars (figures in $ billion): textiles (3.2); iron and steel (2.6); food processing (1.9); paper and printing (1.8); chemicals and allied

---

* This is the number of *wage-earners* in industry. The difference between this figure and that shown for 'Manufacturing' in Table 2 arises from the inclusion in the latter figure of self-employed and salaried workers.

products (1.5); lumber products (1.2). Textiles, it will be noted, still led the way both in employment and value added. If, however, we include with the basic iron and steel industry the further processing of its output into machines and other final products, then this group together surpassed textiles in both respects. Motor manufacturing in 1921 employed about 150,000, slightly fewer than the manufacture of electrical machinery and apparatus, and fewer than the makers of boots and shoes, or of men's clothing or of women's clothing. Already the electrification of American industry had gone far : in 1919 just over 80 per cent of all factories with an annual product of $500 and over were using electrically powered equipment.

Industry was very heavily concentrated geographically in a small number of states. Five states had half a million industrial wage-earners or more, and these accounted for half the total (figures in thousands) : New York (1000); Pennsylvania (864); Massachusetts (579); Illinois (514); Ohio (494). At the other extreme no fewer than thirty-five states had under 100,000 wage-earners and together accounted for only one-fifth of the total. Only two states of the South, North Carolina (136) and Maryland (107), had over 100,000. The remaining fifteen Southern states *together* had under one million industrial wage-earners, i.e. fewer than the one state of New York, or than the two Mid-Western states of Illinois and Ohio.

Although mining appears low on the list in Table 2, it employed more wage-earners than most industries considered separately. Coal-mining alone had 700,000 wage-earners, more than the wood-working industries, the third in size of all industries. The size of this labour force proved to be excessive when the coal industry began to contract in 1920. The other leading extractive occupations after coal-mining were petroleum, iron ore, copper, gold and lead.

The year 1920 saw an important legal decision affecting the structure of American industries. In several cases before the war the trust-busting campaign launched by President Theodore Roosevelt under the Sherman Anti-Trust Act of 1890 had resulted in the dissolution of large corporations, culminating in 1911 in the dissolution of the American Tobacco Company and the Standard Oil Company of New Jersey. Despite the attempt under the Clayton Act of 1914 to give still more teeth to anti-trust policy, the Supreme Court in 1920 did *not* dissolve the United States Steel Corporation, by far the largest industrial corporation since it had become the first billion-dollar corporation on its foundation in 1901. The Court

23

said explicitly, 'the law does not make mere size an offence', even though U.S. Steel was responsible for almost half the nation's total output. Good behaviour, not size, was stated to be the criterion and U.S. Steel was held not to have engaged in the illegal, predatory practices for which American Tobacco and Standard Oil had been condemned.

The U.S. Steel decision left the way clear for the merger movement to continue in the 1920s, providing certain codes of conduct were observed. The evidence suggests that the degree of monopoly control did not increase significantly in the 1920s; indeed it changed little in the half-century after 1905, with the leading ten corporations controlling about 10 per cent of total industrial assets.[1] But the 1920s saw the movement towards industrial concentration taking new forms and new paths, especially in the direction of oligopoly.

One sector of the American economy curiously unaffected by the merger movement was banking, in sharp contrast with the contemporary situation in Britain. Like agriculture, banking was highly atomistic in structure. There were in 1920 no fewer than 30,000 separate banks of which only 500 had branches. The remainder were unitary banks – one office, one bank. Their assets were limited : the national average was under $2 million per bank; but many, especially in agricultural areas, had total assets of under $1 million. These small banks were highly vulnerable. Since they were small separate units, there was no 'lender of last resort' to whom they might turn in times of trouble. There was no central bank comparable to the Bank of England. Under the Federal Reserve System of 1913 twelve Federal Reserve cities had been designated to be the location of the twelve Federal Reserve banks. One of the purposes of the Act was to create greater banking stability. Even in the prosperous 1920s, however, over 5000 banks failed, and of these almost nine out of ten were small county banks with assets of under $1 million.

Membership of the System was not compulsory and in 1920 only 9000 banks were members, though these were in general the larger, sounder institutions. The System had at its centre the Federal Reserve Board but its powers of control were still largely unexplored. There can be little doubt that American banking institutions were still in 1920 an element of great instability in the nation's economy. The significance of that instability will be examined in later sections of this work.

24

2

Common Features of the Inter-war Years

1 THE UNITED STATES IN THE WORLD ECONOMY

If 1929 may be regarded as the Great Divide in American continental history, the First World War has to be so regarded where America's position in the world economy is concerned. Until the First World War the United States was still a net debtor nation; true, she was lending to other nations even before 1900, but she was at the same time continuing to borrow from others and still had a huge accumulation of debt from her nineteenth-century importation of capital. The United States remained a net borrower from the outside world right up to the First World War.

TABLE 3

The American balance of foreign investment

	1908	*1914*	*1919*
		(in $ billion)	
U.S. investment in foreign countries	2.5	3.5*	7.0
Foreign investment in the United States	6.4	7.2	3.3
Net U.S. lending (+) or borrowing (−)	−3.9	−3.7	+3.7

* This was made up of about $2½ billion direct investment (i.e. in American concerns established abroad) and $1 billion 'portfolio' investment. The sum was *less than one-fifth* of the value of Britain's foreign investments at the same date. Nevertheless it represented about 7 per cent of the American G.N.P. in 1914, roughly the same percentage as in the late 1960s.

The First World War completely changed this situation. As Table 3 shows, the figures for 1919 show an almost exact reversal of those for 1914. The United States emerged from the war as the leading creditor nation of the world on current account. The point must be made clear that Britain's *total* foreign holdings, despite the liquidations of the war years, still exceeded America's, but this was largely a passive balance and from 1919 to 1920 the United States had become the major *active* supplier of fresh capital to the rest of the world. In addition to being the leading creditor nation, America was also one of the greatest import markets, one of the largest producers and exporters of many agricultural products, and her economic condition and policy now had a more direct effect on world economic conditions than those of any other country. For the first time the saying was becoming a truism : When America sneezes, the rest of the world catches cold.

II THE TERMS OF TRADE

The world economy between the wars was everywhere characterised by a fairly general condition that the terms of trade were against primary producers. With few exceptions, there appeared to be a glut of raw materials and foodstuffs on the world markets, with consequent low returns for their producers. Although this situation was aggravated by the depression of the thirties, it was nevertheless common to both decades (and to most countries of the world and most commodities in international trade). Industrial products were relatively expensive; primary produce was relatively cheap. This obviously conferred advantages on industrial producers (and Britain was one of the main beneficiaries) but implied great difficulties for food and raw material producers.

The United States' economy shared this international experience, and in consequence the urban–industrial sectors of the economy enjoyed the advantages of relatively cheap food and raw materials throughout the period, while farmers and coal miners (particularly) had difficulty in maintaining their incomes. Obviously there were many inconsistencies : tobacco prices held better than raw cotton prices; meat and fruit prices better than grain prices; oil prices better than coal prices, and so on. The reasons for, and economic consequences of, these features in the terms of trade will constitute an important element in the discussion to follow. Let it suffice for the moment that they were among the features common to both decades.

III AGRICULTURE

It follows directly from the above that most American farmers were confronted with the danger of a fall in their real incomes throughout the inter-war years and that the onset of the depression turned the danger into reality for most and catastrophe for many. Thus throughout both decades one can regard agriculture as a problem sector within the American economy.

The nature of the problem must be carefully defined. It was essentially the problem of the time-and-motion-study expert who (like F. W. Taylor himself), having insisted on payments by results, finally loses his job, precisely because his methods are too successful. The previous quarter century had seen American agriculture develop to a level of efficiency unparalleled in world history and it was this very efficiency which, once demand ceased to expand at its previous rate, resulted in a situation of over-production and falling prices. Between the mid-1890s and 1914, the American farmer had thrived on the rapid expansion of the domestic market. The nineteenth-century peak of exportation was reached for most food items in the late 1890s or in 1900, and the prosperity of the next decade and a half was derived from the expansion of internal demand because of population growth (including immigration) and rapid urbanisation. The First World War added to this the West European demand for American food, and exports again bounded ahead, to reach unprecedented levels in the years 1917–20. All these encouragements caused American farmers to expand their activities and improve their efficiency, above all through mechanisation. With the collapse of the world market and the failure of the domestic market to expand after 1920, the result was a serious glut in important sectors of agriculture. Gradually productive resources began to be moved out of agriculture (and of course the speed with which this occurred was also one of the influences on the demand side) but the process was a slow one, and the most rapid withdrawal has occurred as recently as in the years 1965–72.

The general features of American agriculture between the wars may be summarised as follows :

27

1 Factors influencing supply of agricultural produce

(a) *Labour.* Although the proportion of the American labour force engaged in agriculture declined throughout the nineteenth century (e.g. 1860, 60 per cent; 1910, 30 per cent), as seen earlier, the total number employed in (and the total family members dependent upon) agriculture continued to expand until the First World War.

The inter-war years saw, for the first time in American history, a decline not merely in the relative number, but now also of the absolute number, engaged in American agriculture. But the decline, though real, was nevertheless slow, too slow to redress the balance between the agricultural and other sectors of the economy. A question which must be asked is why the withdrawal was so slow, especially in the 1920s when there were as yet no farm supports to keep farmers farming.

(b) *Land.* Only in a limited sense had the year 1890 seen the 'closing of the frontier' and the acreage of land under cultivation continued to increase during the period of agricultural prosperity. It is possible to define land under cultivation in various ways, but by most definitions the peak was reached somewhere in the decade 1929–39.* The trend is not so obvious in land as in labour, but there is a clear deceleration of the formerly rapid increase of farm acreage in these years.

(c) *Capital.* With labour and land, the nineteenth-century trends were halted but with capital the trend towards intensification continued. Especially in the 1920s American agriculture became more and more highly mechanised. The amount of capital both per worker and per acre increased. Table 5 shows some representative items of farm equipment.

---

* Today's figures show a huge reduction of the agricultural work force to about 3.3 million. 'Land in farms' has increased (owing to the addition of Alaska and Hawaii, and continuing expansion of pasture) but the acreage of cropland is much the same as in 1929–30. There was a reduction of cropland during the early thirties, followed by recovery and then a great increase in the Second World War, but a return thereafter to roughly the pre-war acreage. Hence (among other reasons) the view expressed earlier that 1929 marked the final 'closing' of the frontier as measured by this criterion. Of course, output per acre has increased enormously between 1929 and the present day.

TABLE 4

U.S. farm labour and land, 1890–1940

	1890	1910	1919–20	1929–30	1939–40
Total farm employment (million)	10.0	11.3	11.1	10.5	9.0
Number of farms (million)	4.6	6.4	6.4	6.3	6.1
Land in farms (million acres)	623	879	956	987	1061
Land used (or available) for crops (million acres)	358	478	503	522	530

TABLE 5

Farm equipment, 1910–40

	1910–11	1920	1930	1939–40
		(in thousands)		
Tractors	1	246	920	1545
Motor-trucks	2	139	900	1047
Combine harvesters	1	4	61	190
Corn-pickers	—	10	50	110
Farms with milking machines	12	55	100	175

It will be seen that despite the depression farmers continued to try to make their farms more efficient through capital investment even in the 1930s. Productivity increased not only through mechanisation but also through product diversification, greater application of fertiliser and developments in farm technology such as improvements in seeds.

2 Factors influencing demand for agricultural produce

(a) *Foreign demand.* By 1920 the European nations were beginning to recover from the war and thereafter their imports of food from the United States drastically declined. The value of America's exported foodstuffs (crude and manufactured) had reached a peak of over $2.6 billion in 1919, but slumped to under $1 billion by 1923, averaging $756 million between 1926 and 1930; the lowest figure during the inter-war years was $202 million in 1936 (cf. average 1897–1901 = $535 million; average 1907–11 = $445 million).

(b) *Domestic demand.* Several factors determined the level of internal demand for agricultural products : the rate of population growth in general, and in particular the rate of urban growth (see below, Chapter 3, Section III); the level of industrial demand for industrial raw materials produced by American agriculture; the changing nature of demand for both foodstuffs and raw materials.

Suffice it at this stage to observe that the domestic market did not expand sufficiently to compensate for the loss of foreign markets. Population growth was slowing down; urban growth was slower than in the pre-war period; both affected the potential demand for food and other agricultural produce. Moreover the nature of demand was changing. Synthetic fibres, for example, were beginning to replace raw cotton. One sign of the affluence of the 1920s was a change of dietary habits as people, especially women, began to eat less starchy food; there was in fact a decline in the *per capita* consumption of bread, while Prohibition removed the demand for grain for breweries and distilleries.

IV POPULATION

The rate of American population growth had been gradually slowing down ever since the Civil War, despite the high level of immigration in the decades before the First World War. But between 1910 and 1940 there was a still more decisive decline. In every decade before the Civil War, population had grown at about 34 per cent per decade; the growth rate fell to 25 per cent between 1860 and 1900 and to 20 per cent in the decade 1900–10. After 1910, however, the figures proceed as shown in Table 6.

TABLE 6

Population of the United States, 1910–70

	Total population in millions	Increase in millions	Percentage increase per decade	
1910	92.4			
1920	106.5	14.1	15.2	1910–20
1930	123.2	16.7	15.7	1920–30
1940	132.1	8.9	7.3	1930–40
1950	151.7	19.6	14.8	1940–50
1960	179.3	27.6	18.2	1950–60
1970	203.2	23.9	13.3	1960–70

SOURCE: Official Census figures, from the decennial *Census Reports*.

The components of American population growth are natural increase and immigration, and both were falling during the inter-war years. Immigration declined from 8.8 million in the first decade of the century, to 5.7 milion in the 1910s, 4.1 million in the 1920s and only ½ million in the 1930s. The decline after 1920 was influenced by the Quota Acts of 1921 and 1924, which eventually caused a slump from an annual level of over 800,000 in 1921 to below 180,000 by the late 1920s. By 1940 the proportion of foreign-born in the total population had fallen to 9 per cent, the lowest figure for a century. (From 1860 to 1920 all Censuses had shown a foreign-born percentage of around 14 per cent.)

1 Birth rates and death rates

Various factors influenced the decline in the rate of natural growth, and this is no place to discuss such a complex subject.[1] Both the birth rate and the death rate fell throughout the inter-war years, and in this continuing trend there is no sharp contrast between the twenties and thirties. The birth rate fell from about 28 per thousand in 1920 to 21 per thousand in 1930 and remained below 20 per thousand all through the 1930s. (Figures for annual marriages and the marriage rates are given below, on pp. 35–6.) The death rate continued its steady decline from 13.0 per thousand in 1920 to 10.8 per thousand in 1940; infant mortality (i.e. deaths of live-born infants before the age of one year) fell even more dramatically, from 85.8 per thousand in 1920 to 64.6 per thousand in 1930, and 47.0 per thousand in 1940. In both these respects the 1930s were *better* than the 1920s: average death rate: 1921–8, 11.8 per thousand; 1931–8, 11.0 per thousand; average infant death rate: 1921–8, 76.4 per thousand live births; 1931–8, 62.1 per thousand live births.

Despite the fall in infant mortality, the still greater fall in the birth rate brought a decline in family size. One important social feature of the 1920s was the so-called emancipation of women (or at any rate the first beginnings), and one of its aspects was the deliberate decision to have fewer children, a decision now made possible by better (though still far from satisfactory) methods of birth control.* The total number of births fell, especially in the 1920s (1920, 3.0 million; 1925, 2.9 million; 1930, 2.6 million; 1935, 2.4 million; 1940, 2.6 million), despite the growing number of women of child-bearing age (1920, 24.7 million; 1930, 29.1 million; 1940, 32.0 million).

It is important to note that this decline in family size was still mainly an urban phenomenon, as it had been even in the nineteenth century. Town dwellers were, as never before, confronted by an increasing choice of consumer goods and pleasures, some of which came to be preferred to parenthood.

2 Rural–urban distribution

If one is looking for turning-points, some significance may be attached to the fact that the Census of 1920 showed for the first time in American history that over 50 per cent of the population was 'urban'. This in itself strengthened the tendency towards a declining rate of population growth (because of the tendency of town dwellers to have smaller families). But it would be wrong to jump to the conclusion that by the 1920s the United States had become a characteristically urban society. The American Census definition of

---

* The connection between these developments is well summarised in the immortal *double entendre* of the examination candidate who wrote: 'With the coming of birth control it was no longer necessary for women to be chained to the kitchen sink.'

'urban' is a very low one – merely a place of 2500 inhabitants. If the figures are re-stated, then a rather different picture emerges : even in 1940 over half the American nation still lived either in rural areas or in communities of fewer than 10,000 people.

TABLE 7

Rural population, 1920–40

	% 1920	% 1930	% 1940
Rural	48.8	43.8	43.5
Rural + all places under 5000	52.9	47.7	47.3
Rural + all places under 10,000	57.6	52.5	52.4
Rural + all places under 25,000	64.2	59.9	60.0
Rural + all places under 50,000	69.0	65.1	65.6

Reversing these figures we observe that both in 1930 and 1940 40 per cent of Americans lived in cities larger than 25,000; higher up the scale, under one-quarter lived in cities larger than 250,000, but in 1930 15 million persons (or 12.3 per cent) already inhabited the five large concentrations of over one million inhabitants (New York, 6.9 million; Chicago, 3.4 million; Philadelphia, 2.0 million; Detroit, 1.6 million; Los Angeles, 1.2 million).

In the South in 1930 the urban sector still amounted to only 34 per cent of the total population; i.e. two out of every three Southerners lived in communities of fewer than 2500 persons. This had changed little by 1940, when the urban proportion had merely increased to 37 per cent. As late as 1940 28 states, out of the total of 48, were still over 50 per cent rural; 20 of these were over 60 per cent rural; 10 were over 70 per cent rural; and 5 (Mississippi, North Dakota, South Dakota, South Carolina and Arkansas) were over 75 per cent rural.

3 The black population

More will be said later about other aspects of population growth in the 1920s and 1930s, but two further general demographic observations are still to be made. Firstly, the black proportion of the total population had been declining throughout the nineteenth century and reached its lowest point in the inter-war period, with about 10 per cent of the total. But these years also saw the first significant movement of black people from the South to the cities of the North. This had begun during the decade of the First World War so that when the migrant jazz musicians reached cities like Chicago, they already had the nucleus of a following. The number of black people in Illinois, for example, increased threefold in twenty years, from one-third of a million in 1910 to one million in 1930. Table 8 shows the national figures.

TABLE 8

The American black population, 1910–40

	Total black in millions	Black as percentage of total U.S. population	Total urban black in millions	Urban black as percentage of total black	Increase of urban black in millions	Percentage increase of urban black	
1910	9.8	10.7	2.7	27.5			
1920	10.5	9.9	3.6	34.2	0.9	33	1910–20
1930	11.9	9.7	5.2	43.7	1.6	44	1920–30
1940	12.9	9.8	6.3	48.6	1.1	20	1930–40

The 1920s thus saw the urban black population grow by $1\frac{1}{2}$ million. The black population more than doubled in many major northern cities: in New York from 152,000 to 328,000; in Chicago from 109,000 to 234,000; in Detroit from 41,000 to 120,000.

4 Age structure

The second significant demographic feature of the inter-war years is found in the age structure of the population.

On the one hand, the lengthening of human life increased the number of persons over 65 years of age both absolutely and pro-portionately (1910, 4.1 million; 1920, 5.1 million; 1930, 6.8 million;

1940, 9.0 million; an increase from 4.7 per cent of the total in 1920, to 5.4 per cent in 1930, and 6.9 per cent in 1940). On the other hand, at the other end of the scale, the numbers under 15 years of age increased by only 2.5 million in the 1920s (compared with an increase of 4.1 million in the 1910s) and actually *declined* by 3.1 million in the 1930s. These figures are symptoms of an ageing population. There were in 1940 over 4 million *more* persons over 65 than in 1920 but over half a million *fewer* children under 15 years. The median age thus rose from 25.3 years in 1920 to 26.5 years in 1930 and 29.0 years in 1940; the rural-farm median age was much lower than the urban (22.4 years for white and 18.6 years for black compared with urban figures of 28.6 and 27.4 years in 1930; and in 1940, 25.4 white-farm and 19.8 black-farm compared with 31.3 white-urban and 28.9 black-urban).

The net outcome of these trends was an *increase* in the proportion of the population between the ages of fifteen and sixty-five years, i.e. in the potential work force. The 'productive' section of the population grew from 63.4 per cent of the total population in 1920 to 65.1 per cent in 1930 and 68.1 per cent in 1940. Or, numerically, 'producers' grew by 13 million between 1920 and 1930 while 'dependants' grew by 4 million; and in the 1930s 'producers' grew by 10 million while 'dependants' declined by 1 million.

Space does not permit a full discussion of the economic implications of these data, but they may be interpreted as giving a further impetus to the tendencies towards over-production already present (for other reasons) in the economy. On the other hand, it is generally supposed that the group with the highest propensity to consume is that between the ages of twenty and thirty years, and this age group maintained a fairly constant proportion of the total population (1920, 17.4 per cent; 1930, 16.8 per cent; 1940, 19.1 per cent); in absolute figures it increased by $2\frac{1}{2}$ million in the 1920s and by 2 million in the 1930s. Moreover, the marriage rate (marriages per thousand population, a likely indicator of the creation of new households) remained at a surprisingly constant high level throughout the inter-war period, falling below 10.1 per thousand (the average for the years 1908–12) only in 1928, 1930, 1931, 1932 and 1933;[*] only 1932 (7.9) fell below the marriage rate average (8.7) in the later quinquennium 1960–4. The annual number of marriages averaged 1.2 million in 1920–4, 1.2 million in 1925–9, 1.1 million

[*] The divorce rate also fell during the years 1930–3.

in 1930–4, and rose to 1.4 million in 1935–9. The total number of households increased in every year of the inter-war period, from 24.5 million households in 1920 to 30.0 million in 1930 and 35.2 million in 1940.

Other things being equal, these age, marriage and household data should have given rise to a powerful impetus to private consumption generally and to house building in particular. In this respect at least, demographic factors were favourable for a healthy expansion of the economy based on the domestic demand usually associated with household formation.

V THE CONSEQUENCES OF TECHNOLOGICAL CHANGE

The paradox of agricultural poverty apparently resulting from the improvements in efficiency has already been noted. But similar problems were to be found in other sectors of the economy. The rise of new industries often, indeed usually, carries with it a threat to the existence of old ones. Nowhere was this better seen than in the railroads. No sooner had they reached their peak than at once they began to decline. The arrival of the motor-car and its rapid acceptance in the 1920s brought difficulties to all railroads and disaster to some. Passenger traffic at once began to contract in the 1920s and the number of railroad employees fell by about a quarter of a million between 1920 and 1929. True, the number of electric locomotives about doubled to over 600 (though the number of steam contracted by 7000) and freight carriage held its own more successfully, but the decline of the railroads was unmistakable until the Second World War afforded temporary relief.

As in Britain, other old-established American industries faced the onslaught of new, technologically more advanced industries. The cotton textile industry of New England, and the newer cotton textile industry of the South, both encountered difficulties with the change in clothing fashions and the advent of synthetic fibres. Coal's brief period of supremacy as America's leading source of energy ended (in association with the decline of railroads) as new fuels, especially oil, rose in importance and as coal itself was used more efficiently by being transformed into electricity rather than into steam. Between 1919 and 1929 the quantity of coal needed to generate one kWh of electricity was halved. At the same time the amount required on railroads per train-mile was reduced by one-quarter. Although coal mines had 700,000 workers on their books in the 1920s, they could provide full-time employment for only 500,000.

The new industries themselves had a number of characteristics to be noted. During the first phase of industrialisation, in the United States as in Britain, industries had mainly made the same goods with the same materials but made them more efficiently; now they were constantly offering new, previously unimagined, goods made from new, unknown materials. The motor-car, the radio, the refrigerator, the moving picture, the telephone, were all major and widespread innovations in the lives of most Americans between the wars.

The new industries, moreover, were providing consumer goods which typically could not be bought out of the weekly wage-packet. Also they were durable goods which, once bought, need not, like foodstuffs, be replaced daily or weekly, but which were expected to last if not a lifetime at any rate for several years. The patterns of consumption of large sections of the population were changing rapidly, with a growing share of income spent not on necessities but on luxuries; while of course almost as rapidly, the luxuries of yesterday became the necessities of today. This increase in 'discretionary' expenditure became a continuing feature in American (and later British) life.

Another important characteristic of the new industries was that they typically did not develop in isolation, but attached to themselves the fortunes of many other sectors of the economy. The new industries, in other words, took part in a process that has been described as 'block development'. The American motor-car industry is one of the best examples of such block development. Its raw material supply required the growth of the metal industries, rubber, glass, upholstery, springs, electrical parts and so forth. The production and distribution of petrol and oil also developed with the motor-car industry (and the 1920s saw the innovation in the United States of that accepted part of the twentieth-century landscape, the 'gas' station). Finally, to permit the operation of motor-cars, road building was undertaken on an unprecedented scale (and this in turn greatly increased governmental activity), and with roads and cars many essential service industries grew up. By the mid-1920s the American automobile industry was providing employment for 7 per cent of the total work force and consumed 15 per cent of the total steel output.

This increased interdependence in growth also involved a more widespread danger of contraction in depression. For good and bad, large sectors of economic life had come to be tied to the fortunes of a few dominant leading industries. Further, this increased interdependence was responsible in the long run, more than any other single factor, for the eventual enormous increase (mainly after 1940) in the power of labour, as it gradually became apparent that even a small strike, by a mere handful of workers, might paralyse activity throughout a large, complex area of economic operations.

The new industries were also characterised by the application of mass-production methods on a large scale. They were generally organised as large corporations, employing large amounts of capital. Until the First World War it was generally true that the value of machinery in productive processes increased more rapidly than the value of output, i.e. the capital/output ratio increased. After about 1920 the capital equipment itself became more and more efficient and a given quantity of capital produced more and more of the final product. i.e. the capital/output ratio fell. In other words, industries came to require somewhat less capital than previously to create a given output.

Even more significant was the continuing improvement in the productivity of labour. The greatest gains were made in the 1920s when the industrial production per wage-earner rose from an index of 100 in 1921 to 135 in 1927 and 145 in 1929; even the later 1930s saw a slight rise, the index reaching 151 in 1939.

On a different level it is to be noted that technological change introduced time-lags of a different nature. While not yet at the pace of post-1945, technology was already in the 1920s beginning to change more rapidly than the mental capacity of human beings to absorb its implications. A significant aspect of the 1920s may thus be encapsulated as the conflict between the growing twentieth-century technology and the still surviving nineteenth-century ideology.

VI STRUCTURE OF EMPLOYMENT

One consequence of increased labour productivity both in industry and agriculture was a marked shift in the structure of the labour force during this twenty-year period. As observed earlier, the proportion of the labour force engaged in agriculture had been declining throughout America's history, although the absolute numbers continued to grow. Now, following the peak reached during the First World War, the agricultural sector of the labour force declined absolutely as well as relatively, i.e. fewer and fewer farmers were needed to produce enough food for a larger and larger total population.

The trend in manufacturing employment is less clear-cut. Output per worker was about 50 per cent higher in 1940 than in 1920. While the total numbers employed in manufacturing grew steadily, the proportion fell in the twenties but recovered slightly in the thirties.

The main area of growth, however, was indisputably the tertiary sector of the economy, as Table 9 demonstrates. To summarise this Table, employment in primary and secondary activities increased between the wars by under 1½ million, while employment in tertiary

TABLE 9

Employment by sectors in 1920, 1930 and 1940

	Total in millions			Percentage of employed labour force*		
	1920	1930	1940	1920	1930	1940
Agriculture	11.4	10.8	9.6	27.4	22.1	18.0
Mining	1.2	1.2	1.2	3.0	2.5	2.2
Total primary	12.6	12.0	10.8	30.4	24.6	20.2
Manufacturing	11.0	11.2	12.7	26.1	23.0	23.9
Construction	2.2	3.1	3.7	5.3	6.4	6.9
Total secondary	13.2	14.3	16.4	31.4	29.4	30.8
Private services	5.0	7.4	9.2	11.7	15.1	17.3
Trade	4.2	6.2	7.7	9.9	12.7	14.4
Government	1.9	2.4	3.3	4.5	5.0	6.1
Transport and public utilities	3.1	3.3	2.7	7.4	7.0	5.0
Finance	0.9	1.5	1.7	1.9	3.0	3.1
Other	1.3	1.6	1.6	2.8	3.2	3.0
Total tertiary	16.4	22.4	26.1	38.2	46.0	48.9
TOTAL employed, all sectors	42.2	48.8	53.3	100	100	100

* NOTE: It is important to understand that this table does *not* include the unemployed. Figures are given to nearest decimal.

activities increased by almost 10 million. The percentage share of both primary and secondary production fell, but that of the tertiary sector increased considerably. By 1940 almost half the labour force was employed in the services (tertiary) sector of the economy.

VII GOVERNMENT AND THE ECONOMY

It is not usual to regard the Harding and Coolidge – or even the Hoover – administrations as energetically interventionist. It will indeed be argued later that, starting in March 1933, the intrusion of the hands of President F. D. Roosevelt into areas of operation formerly reserved to invisible hands was little short of a revolution; certainly it was a dramatic change of direction. Nevertheless it was preceded by a long period of preparation (including the experience of government intervention during the war).

The quarter-century before 1914 had seen the introduction of a number of important measures, and the creation of several government agencies whose activities were already being developed in the 1920s, before the New Deal brought the federal government into the economy on an unprecedented scale. The creation of the Interstate Commerce Commission (I.C.C.) in 1887, the Sherman Anti-Trust Act of 1890, a series of conservation measures, starting with the Forest Reserves Act of 1891, the creation of the United States Forest Service in 1905 to administer the 150 million acres of forest set aside as National Forests, the creation of the Bureau of Immigration in 1894, the trust-busting activities of Presidents Theodore Roosevelt and William Taft, the Elkins Act of 1903 and the Hepburn Act of 1906 to increase the powers of the I.C.C., the Pure Food and Drug Act of 1906 – these and other measures had increased the role in the economy of the federal government or its agencies. A culmination was reached in 1914 with the creation of the Federal Trade Commission (F.T.C.), the passing of the Clayton Anti-Trust Act, and the establishment of the Federal Reserve System. Although a determined effort was made after the war, as we have seen, to dismantle the wartime apparatus of control, some relics remained, not least the Federal Income Tax introduced in, and remaining permanent since, 1913.

It was, however, the experience of wartime administration in the years 1917–19 that initiated the first major experience of governmental control over the American economy. A new class of public administrators cut their teeth in these years, working in co-operation with the business community. Similarly, a new generation of businessmen came to the fore, like Gerard Swope of General Electric (see below, p. 93), to whom co-operation between government and business, as developed out of war needs, appeared not merely necessary but also desirable. It is essential to the understanding of what was to emerge after 1933 to appreciate that the experience of government intervention in the First World War provided the precedents on which the New Deal could draw. Many of the New Deal administrators – Swope himself, and also Bernard Baruch and Hugh S. Johnson – had been trained in the school of wartime administration during the period of America's direct involvement in the First World War; these men in a sense merely returned to Washington in 1933 to resume tasks they had somewhat reluctantly laid down in 1920.

It is also to be remembered that governmental activity in the United States is not confined to the federal government. (For further elaboration of this point, see Chapter 6, Section I.) The degree of *laissez-faire* is always exaggerated if one examines only the federal government. Often the question was not whether the government should act, but *which* government should act. Consequently it is to be noted that the 1920s saw a considerable increase in the role of state and city governments in both promotional and regulatory activities. The former included the building of some 300,000 miles of state highways to meet the new needs created by the motor-car. The latter included the slow, uneven introduction in different states of a series of welfare measures, ranging from conservation to labour regulations, housing projects, educational improvements and different forms of pensions and compensation schemes.

3

Prosperity 1922–9

Modern youth is prone to melancholy; like Rachel, it refuses to be comforted. . . . Economic forces . . . are by nature malevolent. Every labour-saving device has led to a decline of skill and to an increase of unemployment. . . . When prices rise, wages lag behind and the standard of living falls. . . . If prices fall, . . . this must result in a depression of trade and industry, a fall of wages and unemployment; so that once again the standard of life of the workers falls. (T. S. Ashton, 1951.)

Despite the massive evidence that the living standard of the vast majority of the American population improved in the 1920s, the period has a bad reputation. An economic system can never win: if there is full employment and rising consumption then there is always a high social price to pay; if there is depression the evil consequences are patent for all to see.

It is certainly easy to disparage American life in the 1920s. The decade may be arraigned with a very long list of dire offences:

the *apathy*, of over 27 million persons entitled to vote, but failing to do so, in 1920 and 1924;

the *corruption*, seen in the Teapot Dome scandal (see p. 170) during the presidency of Warren G. Harding;

the *hedonism*, depicted by Scott Fitzgerald and other writers of the period;

the *hypocrisy*, where better expressed than in Bruce Barton's description of Christ as one who 'picked up twelve men from the bottom ranks of society and forged them into an organisation that conquered the world . . . the founder of modern business'?

the *intolerance*, of the post-war anti-Red hysteria, or of the religious fundamentalism manifested in Prohibition, in

W. J. Bryan prosecuting schoolmaster John T. Scopes for
teaching evolution, in the militancy of the Ku Klux Klan;

the racialism, embodied in the Immigration Act of 1924, or in
the boast, even of a 'popular' figure like Al Smith,
when, as Governor of New York State, he was accused
of employing a 'Negro wench' as stenographer, that 'in
the employment of Negroes by the State of New York
under his administration this has been done only to fill
such jobs as they are given in the South, to wit : porters,
janitors, charwomen, etc.';

the smugness and self-satisfaction, described by a French observer as 'almost insufferable. . . . Every American is at
heart an evangelist, be he a Wilson, a Bryan, or a Rocke-
feller. He cannot leave people alone . . . his duty to his
neighbour is to convert, purify and raise him to his own
moral heights';[1]

the violence, exemplified by the K.K.K., and by the bootlegging
and gangsterism provoked by Prohibition;

the xenophobia, of isolationism, high tariffs and immigration
restriction.

Yet there is another side to the picture. First, however, let us
glance briefly at the political background.

I POLITICS IN THE 1920S

The data presented in Table 10 all reveal the Republican ascendancy
throughout this decade. In the presidency, this dominance had begun in 1896, broken only by Woodrow Wilson's victories in 1912
(when the Republicans were divided) and 1916 (by a slender
majority). Nothing more clearly demonstrated the national desire to
return to pre-war 'normalcy' than the Republican landslide victory
of 1920 by the greatest percentage of the two-party votes of any
President in American history;* out of the 34 Senators elected in

---

* F. D. Roosevelt's share of all votes cast in 1936 was 60.8 per cent (compared
with Harding's 60.3 per cent in 1920), but if only the two *major* candidates are
considered then Harding's share in 1920 was 63.8 per cent compared with Roosevelt's share in 1936 of 62.4 per cent. Except in 1928 the 'solid South' maintained
its traditional Democratic allegiance, making the above figures all the more
remarkable. In 1928 the unpopularity in the bible-belt South of the Democratic
candidate, Al Smith, because he was Roman Catholic and 'wet' (opposed to
Prohibition) lost him support in many traditionally Democratic states (see below,
pp. 90–1).

TABLE 10

The election results, 1920–30

A. *The Presidency*

Year*	President	Vice-president	Party	Per cent share of votes cast
1920	Harding	Coolidge†	Rep.	60.3
1924	Coolidge	Dawes	Rep.	54.0
1928	Hoover	Curtis	Rep.	58.2

B. *The Congress*

	Senate			House of Representatives		
	Rep.	*Dem.*	*Other*	*Rep.*	*Dem.*	*Other*
1920	59	37	—	300	132	1
1922	51	43	2	225	207	3
1924	54	40	1	247	183	5
1926	48	47	1	237	193	3
1928	56	39	1	267	163	1
1930	48	47	1	218	216	1

* Elections held in November of year indicated, but period of office began on 4 March of the year following.

† Coolidge succeeded to the presidency following the death of Harding on 2 August 1923.

1920, 25 were Republican (including 10 gains and no losses); in the House the Republican majority of 179 was unprecedented, with 24 states (half the total) returning not one single Democratic Congressman.

The 1920 election was the first in which women voted, but the vote was discouragingly low: only 49 per cent of the electorate voted (compared, for example, with 83 per cent in 1896 and 71 per cent in 1916); the real victor, it was said, was General Grouch, the general post-war disillusionment of the populace. The importance of the Republican majority in Congress should not be exaggerated; no major policy issues divided the tweedledees and the tweedledums. Local problems and attitudes predominated but on the only really live issue, Prohibition, both parties were split, 'dry' in one state (or county, or town), 'wet' in another.

Harding summarised the mood in his diagnosis : 'America's present need is not heroics, but healing; not nostrums, but normalcy; not revolution, but restoration; not agitation, but adjustment; not surgery, but serenity; not the dramatic, but the dispassionate; not experiment, but equipoise; not submergençe in internationality, but sustainment in triumphant nationality.'

Harding's successor, Calvin Coolidge, President of the United States from 1923 to 1929, had a philosophy not markedly different, and it is ironical that he above all should be identified with the 'roaring' twenties. An anachronism from decaying rural Vermont, Coolidge presided over the rapid growth of the big super-cities. Shy and frugal to a fault, he occupied the White House through years of bombast and extravagance. With a name Calvin which fitted him like a glove – one wonders at the consequences for civilisation had he been named instead after his dead uncle, Julius Caesar Coolidge – he watched his decade repudiate many aspects of puritanical austerity. A man to whom public speaking was torment, he was in 1924 the first presidential candidate to address the nation by radio, probably talking to the largest audience in human history up to that time. A President whose ideal day was 'one on which nothing happens' – allowing the public to watch him 'at work' in his White House study, engrossed in routine trivia – he tried to ignore the bustling activity and rapid change of the America outside. Sentimental, hypochondriac, vaguely idealistic, prone to irony and self-deprecation, never a joiner or glad-hander, he appears to embody everything that America was *not* in the Coolidge decade.

To those who looked for political change and reform, the main hope rested, not with the opposition 'party, but with a handful of progressive Republican Senators : R. M. La Follette, first father, then son (Wisconsin), E. F. Ladd (North Dakota), G. W. Norris (Nebraska), and later S. W. Brookhart (Iowa), L. J. Frazier (North Dakota), R. B. Howell (Nebraska), and H. Shipstead (Minnesota). It was with these members of their own party that the Republican Presidents had to come to terms in the 1920s.

Some writers have suggested that the real division in attitudes to economic policy lay in the twenties not between the two parties but between President and Congress. Like Harding, his immediate successors followed the precept 'Our most dangerous tendency is to expect too much of government'; the demarcation between 'right' and 'wrong' economic intervention was as clear as that between the roles of President and Congress. The Senate and the House represented *particular*, local interests (and their members depended for votes on their success in safeguarding those interests); the result, if unbridled, would be an extravaganza of log-rolling, pork-barrel politics. The President should by contrast be above such local pressures and considerations and represent the *general*, national interest. During the twenties a growing number of members of Congress wanted the federal government to step in whenever and wherever distress occurred, and to do so through congressional legislation. Until F. D. Roosevelt, the view of the White House was that self-help, not federal intervention, was the remedy for such problems, except in such emergencies as the Mississippi flood of 1928. In this interpretation the opening months of the New Deal in 1933 may be regarded as the victory of the congressional view over the presidential view, rather than that of one party over the other.

II SOCIAL IMPROVEMENT

> The one really new gospel we have introduced is the revelation, after centuries of passively endured privations, that a man may at last free himself of poverty and, most fantastic innovation of all, that he may actually enjoy his existence. . . .

So wrote André Siegfried, observing the American social scene in the mid-1920s. While fully agreeing that the quantity of goods can never wholly measure the quality of life, it is possible to muster a formidable array of statistics to demonstrate the vast material improvements of the decade. (The growth rates given may be compared with the population growth of 16 per cent between 1920 and 1930. In the comparisons with British data, it should be remembered that the American population was about $2\frac{1}{2}$ times the size of the British population.)

Average hourly earnings in industry rose by around 10 per cent from 66 cents in 1923 to 71 cents in 1926.[2] Price movements are difficult to describe concisely, because of the great fluctuations at the beginning of the decade and the variations between different items (see below, pp. 70–1). If 1923 is taken as the point for comparison, there was approximate stability until 1929; if 1920 is the base year, then prices fell; if 1922, then prices rose. The index of food prices rose but that of most other items, especially household furniture and equipment, fell.

46

The 1920s saw an increase of 25 per cent in the number of residences, from 24 to 30 million, catching up to some extent at least with the back-log created by the heavy immigration of 1900–14 and the neglect of house building during the war years. Food production rose dramatically : milk by half, turkeys by half, butter by 40 per cent, eggs by 30 per cent, chickens by 25 per cent, cheese by 20 per cent – and commercially produced ice cream by 62 per cent, reaching 277 million gallons in 1929.

The rising standard of living is to be seen even more in the widening range of consumer goods and services. The most spectacular was, of course, the increase in the number of private automobiles, from 9 million registered cars in 1920 to 23 million in 1929 (cf. U.K., 2 million); by 1929 there was roughly one car for every 4.5 persons (cf. U.K., one per 50), and only half a million fewer cars than there were married couples with separate households. Surfaced roads increased from 388,000 to 626,000 miles (cf. U.K., 41,000). Telephones increased from 13 to 20 million (cf. U.K., 1.8 million), giving 155 per thousand population in 1927 (with 268 per thousand in California; cf. U.K., 38 per thousand); mileage of telephone wire from 28 million to 70 million (cf. U.K., 8 million); electricity from 41 billion kWh hours generated in 1920 to 97 billion in 1929 (cf. U.K., 17 billion kWh), while in many towns the cost of domestic electricity fell by between one-quarter and one-half. In 1922 60,000 families had a radio; already by 1924 the number was 1.25 million, including half a million farms; by 1929, 10 million families, about 40 per cent of the total, had radios (and, interestingly enough, this figure grew steadily through the depression years : 1930, 13.8 million; 1931, 16.7 million; 1932, 18.5 million; 1933, 19.3 million). The 'kitchen revolution' is seen in the annual sales of vacuum cleaners amounting to $40 million in 1925, electric cookers $20 million in 1927 and refrigeration equipment $167 million in 1929. (These figures confirm the opinion of the examinee who symbolised the 1920s in the Coolidge 'fridge and the Hoover vac. !)

In addition, as Bernstein points out, considerable improvement occurred in such free social services as public libraries, playgrounds, parks and public-health facilities.[3] Estimated expenditure on recreation doubled in the decade 1919–29. In the latter year average weekly cinema attendance was 80 million; in 1930 it was 90 million (a figure otherwise reached only in 1946–8). Other forms of entertainment and sports proliferated; the number of bowling teams, for example, increased ninefold.

Education was an extremely important area of improvement. The total number of university students almost doubled to over 900,000 (cf. U.K., 32,000); that of women students more than doubled, to 350,000 (cf. UK., 9000). The number of students in teachers' colleges grew from 62,000 to 219,000 (an inflated figure, however, part of the increase resulting from a reclassification of institutions). The percentage of the age group 14–17 years in school increased from 26 per cent of the total to 44 per cent (cf. U.K., 16 per cent); the numbers in federally-aided vocational courses grew from 265,000 to 887,000; teachers' salaries rose from an annual average of $871 to $1364 (and over $2000 in New York and California). The number of graduate nurses more than doubled; the number of medical students grew by 50 per cent, from 14,000 to 21,000.

These figures are examples of what amounted to a massive increase in consumption, perhaps greater in total and *per capita* than in any previous decade in American history, and comparable only with the 1950s and 1960s.

One of the few examples of decline was in the consumption of alcohol, because of Prohibition : beer consumption suffered by far the greatest decline, falling to below half the pre-Prohibition level; spirit drinkers fared better, and the (illicit) consumption of spirits may even have increased; estimates suggest that total alcohol consumption in the mid-1920s was about two-thirds of the norm for the years 1911–14.

All in all, it can be said that the bread-and-butter problems of survival of earlier decades were now replaced for a majority by the pursuit of happiness in the form of the traditional minority pursuits of wine, women and song, the former made difficult by Prohibition (but pursued none the less, with the added zest given by illegality), the second aided by the beginnings of female emancipation, politically, socially and sexually, the third strongly promoted by the growth of the entertainment industry, not least via the new media of mass communication, radio and cinema.

Rightly, the automobile is regarded as the symbol *par excellence* of the 1920s. As noted earlier, the industry was a major example of 'block development'. Motor-cars came to represent the embodiment of the durable consumer good, and their marketing pioneered, and became dependent on, instalment sales. They gave the farmer a means of transport, both of himself and his goods; and it is not accidental that the early growth of the industry was in part an extension of the industries producing equipment for farmers. The impact of the motor-car on social life was immense.* Its near-relatives, the truck and public bus, emerged in the 1920s to make their own contributions. The American high school, for example, the prototype of the comprehensive school, developed in the 1920s essentially as a function of transport, since the school bus made possible the collection of large numbers of children from wide areas. The school bus gradually brought an end to the rural single-roomed school-house and began an educational experiment eventually to culminate in today's problems associated with school integration and the artificial 'bussing' of children across cities.

It took an outside observer, André Siegfried (whose words headed this section), to appreciate the magnitude of the improvement which had transformed American society and created a vast gulf between American and European living standards. In *America Comes of Age* (1927), Siegfried commented :

A workman is far better paid in America than anywhere else in the world, and his standard of living is enormously higher. This difference, which was noticeable before the War, has been greatly accentuated since, and is now the chief contrast between the old and the new continent. . . . North America, including Canada, is overflowing with abundance and enjoys a standard of living quite distinct from that of Europe. . . . It is impossible to realize it fully until one sees it with one's own eyes. . . . European luxuries are often necessities in America. . . . One could feed a whole country in the Old World on what America wastes. American ideas of extravagance, comfort and frugality are entirely different from European. . . . In America the daily life of the majority is conceived on a scale that is reserved for the privi-

* John Steinbeck, in *Cannery Row*, summarised some of its effects as follows: 'Someone should write an erudite essay on the moral, physical and aesthetic effect of the Model T Ford on the American nation. Two generations of Americans knew more about the Ford coil than the clitoris, about the planetary system of gears than the solar system of stars. With the Model T, part of the concept of private property disappeared. Pliers ceased to be privately owned and a tyre-pump belonged to the last man who had picked it up. Most of the babies of the period were conceived in Model T Fords and not a few born in them. The theory of the Anglo-Saxon home became so warped that it never quite recovered.'

leged classes anywhere else. . . . It is not too much to say that practically all houses are equipped with what in France is called *comfort moderne*. Bathrooms and central heating are considered so indispensable that no one would rent a house without them. . . . It is quite common to find a working-class family in which the father has his own car, and the grown-up sons have one apiece as well. . . . Three or four years ago Europe marvelled at the idea of working-men going to the factory in their own motor-cars, but it never attracted any attention in America. To the American, Europe is a land of paupers, and Asia a continent of starving wretches. Luxury in everyday consumption and the extension to many [of] living conditions previously reserved for the few – these are new phenomena in the history of mankind. . . .[4]

It should be added that not all Siegfried's analysis was favourable. He saw a 'materialistic society, organized to produce things rather than people, with output set up as a god. . . . "Fordism", the very essence of American industry, results in the standardization of the workman himself' (pp. 348–9).

III URBANISATION

As seen earlier the rate of growth of the American population recovered only slightly from the unprecedentedly (in American experience) low level of the previous war decade, and at 16 per cent was considerably lower than that of the 1900s and earlier decades. Despite the Quota Acts of 1921 and 1924, immigration during the decade amounted to 4.1 million, i.e. almost one-quarter of the total growth of 17.3 million. The main element in the decline was the fall in the birth rate.

Here we have a paradox. Although towns were growing, this decline in the birth rate was primarily an urban phenomenon. It is therefore to the towns that we must turn our attention. The popular image of the twenties, created largely by literature and early moving films, is of a nation dominated by the city; as if America awakened one morning and suddenly found herself an urbanised society.

Figures given earlier have already indicated that the extent of urbanisation should not be exaggerated, even as late as 1940. Indeed, quite contrary to the popular image, *towns grew at a slower rate in the 1920s than in any previous decade in American history.** Total urban population increased in the 1920s by 27 per cent, compared with increases in the three previous decades of 36, 38 and 29 per cent respectively. Of course these *rates* represent absolute figures which were rising but, as Table 11 shows, there was no growth (but a slight fall) in the increase of the population of towns under one-quarter of a million (which grew from 1900 to 1910 by 7 million; 1910–20 by 6.9 million, and 1920–30 by 6.8 million). The cities which grew most in the 1920s were the giants : 8 million more people lived in places of over one-quarter of a million in 1930 than in 1920, 5 million more in places of over one million.

The slackening of the growth rate of the smaller cities, the Middletown† – so often held to typify the decade – was very marked, as Table 11 shows. Warren Harding's Marion, Ohio, for example, grew (in thousands) by 3.8 (or 48 per cent) from 1890 to 1900, 6.4 (54 per cent) from 1900 to 1910, 9.7 (or 53 per cent) from 1910 to 1920, but in the 1920s increased by only 11 per cent (from 28,000 to 31,000).

The deceleration in the rate of urban growth is most marked in towns between 100,000 and 250,000, but all sizes below one-quarter of a million show a decline in percentage growth, and some a decline in absolute growth, compared with the preceding decade or decades. A counterpart is seen in the slight *increase* in the rate of growth of the rural population, however paradoxical this may seem, in the 1920s. This failure of the smaller towns to continue their former rate of expansion is an important key to the rural distress of the period. Large numbers of these small communities, sometimes no more than villages or market-towns, afforded farmers both with nearby markets and with their nearest escape-valve in times of

---

* To justify this sweeping assertion, let the figures be given: the percentage increases in urban population in the decade between each Census were as follows:

1790–1800: 60	1840–50: 92	1890–1900: 36
1800–10: 63	1850–60: 75	1900–10: 38
1810–20: 32	1860–70: 59	1910–20: 29
1820–30: 63	1870–80: 43	1920–30: 27
1830–40: 64	1880–90: 57	

† *Middletown* was the title of a famous sociological study by Robert and Helen Lynd, published in 1924. It was a study of Muncie, Indiana, a town of 36,000 in 1920 growing by 27 per cent in the 1920s to 46,000 in 1930 (slightly above the average growth rate of towns of 25,000–50,000 population, which was 25 per cent in the 1920s.

Table II

U.S. urban population, 1900–40

	Population (millions)					Increase (millions)				Increase (%)			
	1900	1910	1920	1930	1940	00–10	10–20	20–30	30–40	00–10	10–20	20–30	30–40
Total urban	30	42	54	69	74	12	12	15	5	38	29	27	8
1 million and over	6.4	8.5	10.1	15.1*	15.9	2.1	1.6	5.0*	0.8	31	19	50*	5
Total over 250,000	10.9	15.4	20.8	28.9	30.2	4.5	5.4	8.1	1.3	41	35	38	5
100,000–250,000	3.3	4.8	6.5	7.5	7.8	1.5	1.7	1.0	0.3	45	35	15	4
50,000–100,000	2.7	4.2	5.3	6.5	7.3	1.5	1.1	1.2	0.6	55	26	23	9
2500–50,000	13.4	17.4	21.5	26.1	29.1	4.0	4.1	4.6	3.0	30	23	21	11
Total 2500–250,000	19.4	26.4	33.3	40.1	44.2	7.0	6.9	6.8	3.9	36	26	20	10
Total rural	46	50	52	54	57	4.2	1.5	2.3	3.4	8	3	5	6

* Figure partly affected by statistical redefinition.

financial difficulty. The farmer's welfare depended primarily on the income he could obtain from the sale of his produce, but also was affected by job opportunities for his family in any small town within reach.

More investigation would be needed before firm reasons could be given to explain adequately this deceleration of the growth of the small towns (which again proceeded apace after 1945).

At the other end of the scale, however, there can be no doubt about the dramatic burgeoning of what has been termed 'the metropolitan super-city'[5] in the 1920s. New York increased by almost $1\frac{1}{2}$ million to reach almost 7 million; Chicago grew to $3\frac{1}{2}$ million; Detroit more than doubled to $1\frac{1}{2}$ million; Los Angeles doubled to reach 1.2 million. The 1920s was the great period of skyscraper-building: almost 400 of them (counted as buildings with over twenty storeys) by the end of the decade, culminating in the completion of New York's Empire State Building in 1930; architecture, as has been said, not for men but for masses.[6]

It was particularly the growth of these giants that polarised the old rural–urban conflict in American life. The soul-less cities, these monstrosities, embodied all Jefferson's fears of urban existence, and much more was now added through their sheer size. Agrarian Fundamentalism still lay at the root of many of the problems of the decade: Prohibition, immigration restriction, political corruption, the role of government. The view was well stated by Walter Lippmann:

Prohibition, the Ku Klux Klan, Fundamentalism, and *xenophobia* are an extreme but authentic expression of the politics, the social outlook, and the religion of the older American village civilization making its last stand against what looks to it like an alien invasion. The alien invasion is in fact the new America produced by the growth and the prosperity of America.

The evil which the old-fashioned preachers ascribe to the Pope, to Babylon, to atheists, and to the Devil is simply the new urban civilization, with its irresistible economic and scientific and mass power. The Pope, the Devil, jazz, the bootleggers, are a mythology which expresses symbolically the impact of a vast and dreaded social change. The change is real enough. The language in which it is discussed is preposterous only as all mythology is preposterous if you accept it literally. The mythology of the Ku Klux Klan is a kind of primitive science, an animistic and dramatized projection of the fears of a large section of our people who have yet to accommodate themselves to the strange new social order which has arisen in their midst.[7]

The notion still died hard (and is still alive in some radical movements of today) that innocence, 'real' values, honesty, integrity, independence and justice can only exist in the rural life-style. The growth of the super-cities emphasised all the fears of urban corruption and dehumanisation. Already in 1922 Lewis Mumford was writing: 'if metropolitanism continues they [our cities] are probably destined to fall by its weight'.

If one seeks the symbol of urban growth in the 1920s, it is to be found in residential and industrial suburbia. The automobile (and road building), the telephone and cheap electricity all stimulated a centrifugal movement which resulted in a far more rapid growth of the 'metropolitan rings' outside city centres, than of inner cities. This movement without doubt brought relief to the former intense congestion of the city centres. Individual home ownership grew and large numbers of people endeavoured to enjoy the best of both worlds, urban affluence in a semi-rural environment.

Another aspect of the population data confirms the view that the heart of America in the 1920s still belonged to Daddy Jefferson. The city, perhaps more than ever, was an alien excrescence with only a minority of its inhabitants being 'true' Americans in the sense that they were themselves born in America of two parents who were themselves American-born. In New York, for example, both in 1920 and 1930 *only one inhabitant in five* was a native-born American of native parentage; 35 per cent were foreign-born; 33 per cent were American-born of foreign parents; 8 per cent had one American parent. This story was repeated (though nowhere else so emphatically) in city after city (and especially in the bigger ones) as the examples in Table 12 show.

A few exceptions might be given at the other extreme, but these are mainly situated in the South. Dallas, Fort Worth, Indianapolis and Reading (Pennsylvania) were the only cities with over 70 per cent native-born of native parentage; Akron, Atlanta, Columbus, Dayton, Des Moines, Kansas City, Nashville, and Richmond were the only cities with over 60 per cent. Birmingham (Alabama) and Norfolk (Virginia) were almost 40 per cent black. Washington D.C.

TABLE 12

Population of certain cities in 1920
(Figure in brackets shows percentage in 1930 to demonstrate
increase in 1920s)

City	Total population	American-born of American parents %	Foreign-born %	American-born of foreign parents %	American-born of mixed parents %	Negro %
New York	6.9 (m.)	21	35	33	8	3 (5)
Chicago	3.4 (m.)	24	30	33	9	4 (7)
Philadelphia	2.0 (m.)	38	22	25	8	7 (11)
San Francisco	0.5 (m.)	33	28	25	11	1 (1)
Boston	0.7 (m.)	24	32	32	10	2 (3)
Detroit	1.0 (m.)	32	29	25	10	4 (8)
New Bedford (Mass.)	121 (000)	17	39	30	9	4 (4)
Lowell (Mass.)	113 (000)	22	34	33	11	—
Milwaukee	0.5 (m.)	29	24	33	13	1 (1)
Fall River	120 (000)	16	35	38	11	—

was just about the purest American city in the nation : 55 per cent
white all-American, 25 per cent black all-American (leaving only
7 per cent foreign-born, and 13 per cent of foreign or mixed parentage).

IV ECONOMIC EXPANSION

Despite the blemishes in some sectors of the economy, the years
1922–9 constitute one of the longest periods of sustained prosperity
in American history. Profits, wages and employment all increased,
and to contemporary observers there appeared to be no reason why
the advance should not continue indefinitely. Economists, businessmen and journalists spoke of a new era and believed the millennium
to be at hand.

Figures given earlier showed that America's G.N.P. (in constant
dollars) rose from $76 billion in 1922 to $104 billion in 1929, a
38 per cent real increase over a seven-year period, or over 5 per
cent per year. In the four years 1923–6 the annual growth rate averaged 7 per cent. The *per capita* growth rate was lower, but still

spectacular : $3\frac{3}{4}$ per cent per year in the seven years 1923–9 and about 5 per cent in the four years 1923–6.

Of the items within the G.N.P. industrial production naturally attracts the most attention. Between 1923 and 1929 the index of manufacturing production rose by almost 30 per cent. The size of the work force in manufacturing was almost constant between those dates. Output per worker increased by almost 30 per cent, despite generally shorter working hours – a remarkable growth of productivity resulting from a wide range of technological innovations. Industrial wages during this period rose by about 45 per cent, the main gains being in the early years.

Nevertheless it would be misleading to imply that the only – or even the main – economic dynamism of the decade was located in the industrial sector. Using the widest possible definition of industrial 'working-class' employment, we find a growth of 1.8 million between 1920 and 1930 (compared with 3 million between 1900 and 1910), from 12.1 to 13.9 million, just enough to maintain such workers as a constant 29 per cent of the total labour force. Meanwhile the total labour force expanded from 42.2 to 48.7 million. Four million of the increase occurred in the tertiary sector of the economy, i.e. among 'white-collar' workers. 'Sales workers' increased by 50 per cent, 'service workers' by 45 per cent, professionals and technicians by 45 per cent and clerical (and similar) workers by 29 per cent.

This confirms the view given earlier that the main growth areas in the labour force were in the middle- and lower-middle-class groups rather than in the working-class sector and is further evidence of the proposition that the main urban growth occurred in the giant commercial cities (rather than in the smaller industrial ones) and that the expanding community was predominantly middle-class suburbia.

The main industrial growth sectors are easily identified : the construction industries; the automobile and associated industries; the electricity and electrical-equipment industries; industries producing machinery of all kinds; food-processing industries. With the exception of building, all the expanding areas were capital-intensive and the growth in their output was not matched by a proportionate expansion of their work force. Within that work force, the emphasis was shifted by mechanisation and mass-production techniques towards a greater proportion of unskilled workers. This change of

TABLE 13

Indexes of economic expansion, 1922–9

Year	G.N.P. (at constant prices) Total (1922=100)	G.N.P. (at constant prices) Per capita (1922=100)	Output Per man-hour in manufacturing (1922=100)	Output Per worker in agriculture (1922=100)	Construction Total value (1922=100)	Construction Residential value (1922=100)	Automobiles car sales in millions	Automobiles Truck and bus sales in thousands
1922	100	100	100	100	100	100	2.3	270
1923	113	111	98	103	129	131	3.6	409
1924	117	112	105	105	143	151	3.2	417
1925	119	113	112	111	156	164	3.7	531
1926	127	119	115	115	167	167	3.7	609
1927	128	119	118	111	161	154	2.9	465
1928	130	119	124	115	154	142	3.8	583
1929	138	124	129	115	139	108	4.5	882

SOURCE: Calculations on indexes based on data from the *Historical Statistics of the United States*.

emphasis in turn had consequences for the trade-union movement which was still attempting, under Samuel Gompers, to restrict union membership to skilled workers. While the middle ranks of society were moving together in the process of *embourgeoisement*, a new solid core of proletarian, unskilled industrial wage-earners was coming into being.

Table 13 provides certain selected data for these years to illustrate the main trends; other data will be given in later sections in the examination of particular aspects of the situation.

Although the trends indicated are in most respects obviously upward, the progress is not a smooth one. The G.N.P. figures show that the main increase occurred in three sharp spurts: 1922–4, 1925–6 and 1927–9. The variations in the rate of growth have sometimes been taken to represent two minor cycles, with retardation in 1924–5 and 1926–7, with the last expansion seen as the first phase of a third minor cycle.

The most important feature to be observed is that while the construction index and automobile sales both fell in 1927, reflecting the general retardation of growth in that year, automobile sales increased rapidly during the final expansion of 1928 and 1929, but construction continued to decline. The figures must be kept in perspective, however, despite this decline; total new construction even in 1929 was double the 1918–19 level and about three times the average of 1906–14; in other words building was still very active. Nevertheless, it would seem that the expansion of that sector of the economy concerned with investment in building does appear to have reached its peak in 1925 or 1926; while public construction expanded throughout, business construction became stable in 1927; residential construction began to decline as early as 1925, slowly at first but with gathering momentum, as can be seen from the fact that in 1929 it was only 8 per cent above the 1922 level. The first important drag on the economy to be felt during this generally expansive trend was this downward movement of residential construction in these closing years.

For the rest, the last two years of the expansion saw a steady, sustained growth of consumption and a stabilisation of employment (see below, p. 69). They also saw the development of that speculative boom which reached its climax in the summer and autumn of 1929 and culminated in the Wall Street crash which will be examined later in this chapter (pp. 74–6).

The next task is to analyse more carefully certain features of the prosperity of the twenties and to probe more deeply into some of the weaknesses beneath the surface. The specific question to be asked is whether these underlying weaknesses can be held responsible for the eventual catastrophic collapse of the economy in the depression years.

V ARE THE CAUSES OF THE GREAT DEPRESSION TO BE FOUND IN THE PROSPERITY OF THE 1920s?

In approaching this question we may employ a useful frame of reference by attempting to distinguish between three different types of phenomena : economic, institutional and political. The first includes those elements in the situation that relate above all to the changes which occurred in the economic circumstances of the time : changes in the allocation of the means of production to different sectors of the economy, productivity, the patterns of consumption and the distribution of wealth and incomes. The second includes the institutions and practices inherited from the past, e.g. the structure of banking, trade unions. The third primarily concerns the policy decisions taken at different times, by different persons in authority (primarily but not exclusively governmental) in different areas affecting the economy. The decisions themselves must include several made primarily or even exclusively for non-economic reasons, but with important consequences for the economy. Prohibition is an example of such a non-economic policy which had important economic consequences.

The framework provided by this threefold categorisation cannot be rigid; there will be some overlap between the categories. Nor can it be made to fit rigidly into a time-period; there will be both continuities and discontinuities between the twenties and the thirties.

1 Economic conditions

(a) *Agriculture.* American farmers, being typically owner-occupiers and having no landlords to provide their capital, had financed the expansion of their farms and equipment during the First World War by borrowing, often in conditions of inadequate loan facilities. When, after the boom, farm incomes failed to share the general rise in the national income, the burden of their debts became increasingly serious to farmers. Production and, in some areas, acreage both continued to expand, however, and farmers went into still greater debt, borrowing a further 20 per cent in the course of the decade, mainly from local banks. The fate of the farmers and these local banks were, as they had been throughout American history, closely connected, a fact of increasing importance during the twenties.

The fall in farm prices generally was serious in the 1920s but not catastrophic, at least until 1928 when a particularly abundant harvest initiated the most serious price fall of the decade. From an index of 217 in 1919 (parity 1910–14=100), prices received by farmers slumped to 124 in 1921, recovered to 142 by 1923, reaching 148 in 1929. Within this composite index grain prices were the most volatile, falling from 235 in 1920 to 121 in 1921, recovering to 156 in 1923 but remaining unstable until a fall to 142 in 1928 and 135 in 1929. Livestock prices were rather more stable; after the initial fall from 206 in 1919 to 127 in 1922 they improved annually, reaching 159 in 1929.

As already observed the labour force in agriculture was reduced during the 1920s. Between 1922 and 1929 some 2 million left the land annually, but many returned and the net loss of total farm population (i.e. including families) in the decade was only 3.7 per cent, from 31.6 million in 1920 to 30.4 million in 1930. Given the economic weakness of primary producers, this movement out of agriculture was not rapid enough to maintain a suitable balance between agricultural production and the demand for agricultural products, even though the non-farm population grew by one-quarter in those same ten years.

The slowness of the movement out of agriculture is not entirely explicable in economic terms alone. The first point to remember is that farm families were generally larger than urban ones. Given the high and growing productivity of agriculture, it was economically necessary for all but one son in every farm family (and, to bring about an eventual reduction, none in some families) to find jobs away from the farm. In a farm family of, say, two sons and two daughters, the economic situation could allow only one member at the most to stay on in agriculture (for example, by taking over the parental farm), if agriculture was to avoid a permanent overproduction crisis; the remaining children needed to find their livelihood elsewhere. The ability of proximate towns to absorb the 'surplus' farm labour generated by the combination of relatively high biological productivity with high agricultural productivity was thus crucial. It is therefore important to recall other facts from earlier sections of this chapter. Firstly, industrial productivity was growing so rapidly that a constant labour force was able to produce a much larger output (to put this conversely, a given output required some 30 per cent less labour in 1929 than in 1920); secondly, the main growth occupationally was in the tertiary sector of the economy, where a certain level of education (which many rural children did not achieve) was often required, not in the unskilled industrial sector; and thirdly, that the medium- and small-sized towns, those to which farmers or their sons and daughters would be the most likely to turn for non-agricultural jobs, were the ones growing least rapidly throughout the inter-war years.

But rural inertia probably had even deeper roots. Agriculture still was regarded as the way of life farmers preferred despite the difficulty of maintaining their incomes. Yet their memories of good times were still very fresh. The Golden Age of agricultural prosperity which had lasted for the quarter-century before 1920 was not long past and, in common with most workers when depression strikes, farmers continued to believe optimistically that good times were bound to return if they waited long enough and produced still more in the meantime.

If we turn from labour to land inputs we find that, for many crops, acreage was expanded in the twenties, despite the prevailing conditions of agrarian gloom. Wheat acreage, for example, was higher in 1929 than in any previous year apart from those at the close of the First World War; it was 15 million acres above the 1909–13 average and 11 million acres above the 1924 figure. An important part of that expansion occurred at the end of the war and through the twenties at the 'New Frontier', in the marginal lands of western states such as Kansas, Oklahoma and Western Texas. It was in this same region that the onset of prolonged drought in the early 1930s led to the notorious dust-storms and the creation of the problem of the Dustbowl where roughly one-half of the land was ruined by erosion.

(b) *Industrial employment.* It is a normal pattern of economic growth that as new industries rise old ones decline, with resultant unemployment, under-employment and hardship for the victims of progress. Part of the cost of improved efficiency is the displacement of the less efficient.

We have already identified a number of areas of the American economy where such difficulties were present : railroads, coal, textiles. These structural stresses at particular points may even be regarded as evidence of dynamism in conditions generally. But it was small consolation to the persons and localities which suffered that their problems were caused by the very growth and prosperity they could not themselves enjoy.

As has been observed earlier, the total number of industrial workers showed no significant increase during the 1920s but this fact should not be allowed to conceal shifts between industries and, more importantly, between regions. The greatest expansion in the work force occurred in the production of machinery where the number of wage-earners rose by almost 200,000 between 1923 and 1929. Food manufacturing also increased its labour force by some 50,000. The greatest reduction in manpower occurred in the railroad-associated industries.

The geographical shift of industrial employment has to be considered together with the wide variation in industrial wages in the 1920s. A very wide gulf separated the states with the lowest average industrial wages from those with the highest; in 1923, for example, 170,000 industrial wage-earners in North Carolina averaged $734 per annum, about half the average income of the 250,000 wage-earners in California with $1435. This gap did not narrow in the 1920s and may indeed have widened slightly as wages generally increased more in the high-wage states than in the low-wage states.

With the exception of the Pacific and Mid-western states, the trend was for industrial employment to shift from high-wage to low-wage regions. In particular, the number of industrial wage-earners declined both in New England and the Middle Atlantic states, while increasing in the South Atlantic states. The data are given in Table 14 which also indicates average industrial wages in 1927 in each region.

This tendency of industry to move towards the low-wage regions may be demonstrated in textiles, one of the 'problem' industries but still the largest industrial employer. The total number of wage-earners in textiles remained almost constant, but the centre of the industry moved from New England to the South Atlantic. As Table 15 shows, the four leading New England cotton-manufacturing

TABLE 14

Regional changes in industrial employment in the 1920s

	Total industrial wage-earners in thousands			Increase		Average annual wage in dollars
	1919	*1923*	*1929*	*1919–29*	*1923–9*	*1927*
East North Central	2396	2387	2540	+ 144	+ 153	1446
South Atlantic	817	832	909	+ 92	+ 77	904
Pacific	435	420	470	+ 35	+ 50	1413
West North Central	500	469	471	− 29	+ 2	1229
All other states	723	718	774	+ 51	+ 56	963
Middle Atlantic	2873	2694	2560	−313	−134	1415
New England	1351	1254	1098	−253	−166	1226
Total United States	9095	8774	8822	−273	+ 48	1209

SOURCE: *Statistical Abstract of the United States*, various dates; *Census of Manufactures*, 1923, 1925, 1927, 1929, 1931.

TABLE 15

Employment and wages in cotton manufacturing,
New England and South Atlantic compared, 1919 and 1929

	Number of wage-earners in thousands				Average annual wage in dollars		
	1919	*1929*	*Change 1919–29*		*1919*	*1929*	*Change 1919–29*
Massachusetts	122*	71	− 52		897	926	+ 3%
Rhode Island	31	22	− 10		922	997	+ 8%
New Hampshire	21	14	− 7		856	902	+ 5%
Connecticut	16	11	− 5		945	994	+ 5%
Total	191	117	− 74	Av.	901	943	+ 5%
North Carolina	67	92	+ 25		730	662	− 9%
South Carolina	48	72	+ 24		757	652	−14%
Georgia	38	56	+ 18		686	633	− 8%
Alabama	18	28	+ 10		627	609	− 3%
Total	172	247	+ 75	Av.	717	646	−10%

SOURCE: *Census of Manufactures*, 1919–29.

* All figures shown to nearest thousand.

63

states had 74,000 fewer wage-earners in the industry in 1929 than in 1919, while the four leading Southern states increased their work force by 75,000. That is to say, the number of cotton operatives with annual wages approaching $1000 fell while the number with annual wages around $700 increased sharply. Within the Southern states the wage differentials narrowed (the smallest reduction being in the state with the lowest wages in 1919, the greatest in the highest-wage states) but, as the final column of Table 15 shows, the gap between the two regions widened quite sharply since the average wage increased in New England but actually fell in the Southern states. It should be added that the apparent fall in wages in the South does not appear if 1921 is used as the first year instead of 1919.

(c) *The areas of industrial expansion.* The main industrial growth of the 1920s was in the production of goods which lasted for a long time and were luxuries rather than necessities (the so-called durable-use consumer goods). They had two significant characteristics : their purchase was postponable; and their price was too high to be met out of the weekly wage packet.

The first characteristic meant that, once the initial purchase had been made, subsequent purchases would be for replacement; and, when times were bad, people put off replacing such items of equipment as motor-cars, household apparatus and so on as long as possible – and if times were bad enough did not replace them at all.

The second characteristic required the development of a new method of payment. The goods were indivisible (a motor-car could not be bought one wheel at a time) but the payments were not necessarily so (a customer could offer to pay a few dollars at a time). The twenties saw a vast extension of the system of buying by fractional payments, i.e. by instalments or on the 'never-never'. In effect this meant that large numbers of people went into debt to buy the new industrial products. These debts subsequently required repayment of interest and capital. When incomes fell after 1929, this repayment became difficult (or impossible) and potential buyers were reluctant (or unable) to undertake any further instalment purchases.

So long as confidence lasted, it was possible for the new industries to expand rapidly and total purchases could exceed current incomes. But the new industries were extremely vulnerable on both

64

grounds once confidence was lost : customers decided to postpone their purchases, and the system of credit-buying collapsed, leaving incidentally a large hangover of unpaid debts.

(d) *Income distribution.* To many writers this is the most crucial consideration, but many assertions are made without the full appreciation of the complexities of any complete analysis of income distribution.[8] Calculations reproduced in the *Historical Statistics of the United States* have often been quoted, showing, for example, that the richest 5 per cent of the nation received 23 per cent of total incomes in 1923 and 27 per cent in 1928,[9] with 82 per cent of all income from dividends going to that top 5 per cent and 71 per cent of dividends going to the top 1 per cent. From this it is concluded that a redistribution of income occurred in favour of the rich. But the problem is much more complicated. All conclusions based on aggregate data involve an enormous downward drag involved in the inclusion of figures for the South, especially in view of the trend noted earlier towards industry's relocation there. The rise in average hourly earnings cited earlier (p. 46) conceals very great differentials according to occupation, region, age and sex.[10]

It is also important to recognise that many other changes were also occurring, above all in the composition of the labour force. The number of women at work increased from 8.2 million in 1920 to 10.4 million in 1930, including an increase of over one million in the number of married women at work (from 1.9 million to 3.1 million), generally providing second incomes in a possibly childless family. The number of young people at work by contrast declined; in 1930 only 6 per cent of boys aged from ten to fifteen years and 3 per cent of girls were reported in full-time employment (compared with 25 per cent and 12 per cent twenty years earlier); there were 700,000 more males in the age group 14–19 years in 1930 than in 1920, but 150,000 fewer at work; these data of course reflect the increase in the proportion of teenagers continuing in full-time education.

The evidence is not easy to evaluate. A Brookings Institution study published in 1934, for example, showed that the percentage of total income accounted for by wages, salaries and returns to individual entrepreneurs was higher throughout the 1920s than in preceding years.[11] Between 1923 and 1929 total occupational income increased by some 10 billion dollars, although its percentage declined slightly from 76.8 to 75.2 (with a corresponding increase in returns from investment and 'property in production'). Extracts from the data are given in Table 16.

Total realised income from different sources, 1910–29

Year	Total realised income in billion dollars	Occupational income in billion dollars	Percentages of total realised income		
			Occupational income	Returns on investment and property in production	Returns on property
1910	31.4	22.4	74.9	14.3	10.8
1914	35.6	26.6	74.6	14.3	11.1
1921	63.4	47.5	75.0	12.5	12.5
1923	74.3	57.0	76.8	11.9	11.3
1925	81.9	62.8	76.7	12.5	10.8
1927	85.3	64.9	76.1	13.0	10.9
1929	89.8	67.5	75.2	13.6	11.2

SOURCE: M. Leven *et al.*, *America's Capacity to Consume*, Table 11, p. 159.

On the other hand, within the 'occupational income' items, the wage component was almost stable between 1923 and 1929 and the salaries component rose slightly; both were considerably higher in every year of the 1920s than in any year before 1917.* Taken together, wages and salaries increased by some 45 per cent during the 1920s (between 40 and 50 per cent, depending on whether 1919, 1920 or 1921 are used for comparison), and as a share of total incomes show an increase of about 2 per cent.

* Percentages of total incomes

Years	Wages (average)	Salaries (average)
1909–14	38.6	16.6
1915–19	35.9	16.8
1920–2	43.1	20.0
1923	42.0	19.2
1925	40.5	19.8
1927	41.3	21.7
1928	40.0	22.1
1929	42.1	21.7

There is also evidence, however, of a particular concentration of income at the very top of the scale. The number of income-millionaires rose from 65 persons in 1919 to 513 in 1929; the disposable income of the top 1 per cent grew (to cite the most extreme figures) from 13.1 per cent of the total income in 1923 to 19.1 per cent in 1928. So far as the *very* rich were concerned, the verdict of the Brookings Institution analysis can be accepted: 'It appears that income was being distributed with increasing inequality, particularly in the late years of the period: in the late twenties a larger percentage of the total income was received by the portion of the population having very large incomes than . . . a decade earlier.'[12]

Even so, the argument that income became significantly more maldistributed in the 1920s is not proven. On the whole, it would seem that if broad income groupings are taken, income distribution was not significantly more inegalitarian than in previous decades and comparisons with contemporary Europe, including Britain, suggest that the American income structure was probably more egalitarian.

This does not dispose of the argument however. The test is not whether income distribution became less egalitarian during the 1920s but whether the gains in productivity were being allocated in a manner which would sustain demand at the requisite level. The problem was to create new techniques of mass-consumption to meet the new techniques of mass-production.[13] The crisis to come was, in other words, not the age-old one of shortage but one resulting from a phenomenon new to mankind, *abundance*, aggravated locally by particular problems of structural and technological unemployment.

The abundance created by high productivity might have been passed on either through lower prices, or through work-spreading or higher wages. All these occurred, but not on the scale required to maintain and expand purchasing power at a matching rate. It was not enough for the existing pattern of distribution to be maintained; what the economy (as well as social justice) required was a decided redistribution in favour of the poorer sections of the community. The failure to bring about an adequate redistribution must be attributed on the one hand to a lack of adjustment in traditional attitudes (towards labour and profits), on the other hand to institutional inadequacies and in particular to the strength of the price-fixing bodies compared with the weakness of the wage-bargaining bodies.

The failure to redistribute incomes, especially towards the end of the 1920s, must be held to have been instrumental in holding consumption down below its fullest potential and, by adding to the incomes of the very wealthy, to have increased saving at a time when the economy required even further increases in spending.

(e) *Profits.* The opposite side of the same coin is that, in so far as the productivity gains were not being passed on to the public in lower prices or higher wages, they increased the profits of businesses. In turn, these profits might either be distributed to shareholders (thus adding either to purchasing power or to private saving) or retained by the business to add to its capital equipment. The latter seems to have been an increasingly common practice. Indeed, so much ploughing back of profits occurred that many of the larger corporations became self-financing, gradually achieving independence from the need to borrow capital on the Stock Exchanges.

(f) *Savings and investment.* Although the above trends were not universal, they were characteristic enough to create the situation later diagnosed by J. M. Keynes as over-saving (or under-consumption, with its counterpart over-investment). Not enough of the newly created wealth was passed on to the people who spent rather than saved; not enough of the resultant saving found an outlet in real investment as the big corporations no longer required to borrow.

The result was the accumulation of surplus funds which were used for paper investments but without any corresponding real investment (in turn influenced by the slowing down of the expansion of demand).

(g) *Example of the automobile industry.* By the late 1920s the first demand for motor-cars had been satisfied. Twenty-three million cars were on the roads. The total number of households exceeded the number of cars by 6 million. Further car sales now depended on one of the following : an increase in the incomes of the remaining 6 million househoulds, or a further reduction in the price of a car; a further extension, or easing, of credit facilities; or a decision by existing car-owners either to buy a replacement, or to buy a second car. It can probably be said that by 1929, in the given distribution of income with the given pattern of demand and credit facilities, the market had reached satiation point.

Yet, the price of cars had been steadily reduced, while the wages of auto-workers had steadily risen – but, again, not enough. The automobile corporations invested vast sums in expansion during the twenties. This they did out of profits, without needing to raise the capital on the Stock Exchange.

(*h*) *Unemployment*. It is evident that two kinds of unemployment existed in the 1920s; structural, i.e. the loss of jobs in the declining sectors; and technological, i.e. the loss of jobs through mechanisation. The important questions are, how much unemployment was there, and how long did it take the individual worker to find another job?

Neither question can be satisfactorily answered. There was no 'official' collection of unemployment data and 'guestimates' only are available both for the 1920s and most of the 1930s (see below, p. 137). The figures shown in the *Historical Statistics* are reproduced in Table 17.

TABLE 17

Unemployment in the United States, 1919–29

Year	Unemployment in millions	Percentage of labour force	Year	Unemployment in millions	Percentage of labour force
1919	1.0	2.3	1926	0.9	1.9
1920	1.7	4.0	1927	1.9	4.1
1921	5.0	11.9	1928	2.1	4.4
1922	3.2	7.6	1929	1.6	3.2
1923	1.4	3.2	Av. 1919–29	2.1	4.7
1924	2.4	5.5	Av. 1923–9	1.7	3.8
1925	1.8	4.0	Av. 1926–9	1.6	3.4

SOURCE: *Historical Statistics of the United States*, p. 73.

These figures represent the minimum one can assume, but compare favourably with those for the 'full-employment' period since 1945 (e.g. average unemployment 1949–59, 4.6 per cent; 1959–69, 4.8 per cent). Much higher figures, however, are cited by Irving Bernstein who gives two different estimates for the middle years: 1924, 13 per cent and 7.77 per cent; 1925, 13 per cent and 5.7 per cent; 1926, 11 per cent and 6.3 per cent.[14] He goes on to cite figures of around 10 per cent for specific places and firms at specific dates.

Neither the 'optimistic' nor the 'pessimistic' figures can be regarded as satisfactory. Much depends, for example, on the definition of 'labour force' before the figures purporting to show the percentage unemployed take on any meaning. But above all, the duration of unemployment is unknown and probably unknowable for this period. Unemployment would be expected to be of long duration in the localities where declining industries predominated. But how large the army of unemployables had become – and how unemployable they were – remains a matter of conjecture.

(i) *Productivity and prices*. It has already been observed several times that the 1920s saw a marked improvement in economic efficiency, as measured in the output of labour. Although the productivity gains were common to all sectors of the economy, their magnitude varied considerably. In manufacturing, average output per man increased by over 60 per cent between 1920 and 1929; that is to say, an industrial worker created $160 worth of products in 1929 in the same time he had taken in 1920 to create $100 worth (assuming constant prices). In agriculture, *per capita* production grew much less – by about 6 per cent over the same period of time. Between these extremes, in mining and in the railroads, productivity increased by about 30 per cent.

Given the general buoyancy of the economy, and especially of consumer demand, one might have expected to find rising prices. But this did not occur. Throughout the decade the general price level remained fairly stable and it has usually been assumed that the price stability is attributable, wholly or in part, to the fact that because of improved productivity costs of production were constant or falling.

When prices are examined in greater detail, however, the picture is rather more complicated and even the trends are not quite so easily discernible. Assessment of the trends partly depends on the starting date used for comparison. The general level of wholesale prices was about 1 per cent lower in 1928 and 1929 than in 1921

70

and 1922 but some 30 per cent lower than the 1917–20 average. As Table 18 shows, however, prices to urban consumers were 1 per cent higher in 1929 than in 1922–3, though 5 per cent below 1921 and nearly 20 per cent below 1920.

TABLE 18

*Consumers' Price Index for moderate-income families
in large cities, 1920–9**

(Average 1922–3 = 100)

Year	All items	Food	Clothing	Rent	Fuel, etc.	Home furnish-ings	Miscel-laneous†
1920	119	138	160	83	94	135	100
1921	106	105	123	96	100	114	103
1922	99	98	100	99	99	96	100
1922–3 (av.)	100	100	100	100	100	100	100
1923	101	102	100	101	101	104	100
1924	101	101	99	105	100	102	100
1925	104	109	97	105	101	100	101
1926	105	113	96	104	103	98	102
1927	103	108	94	103	101	95	102
1928	101	107	93	100	99	93	103
1929	101	109	92	98	99	92	104

* Table calculated from Dept of Labor, *Handbook of Labor Statistics*, 1947.
† Includes transport, medical care.

Table 18 shows that the changes in consumer prices were somewhat irregular. The general level rose by some 5 per cent between 1922–3 and 1926 but fell back thereafter. Most prices were lower throughout the 1920s than during the post-war boom of 1920. Clothing and household equipment showed the greatest drop and both continued to decline throughout the decade until in 1929 their price indexes (both at 92) were the lowest calculated for any group. Rents rose until 1924–5 when the effects of the high level of house building in the first years of the decade began to take effect. Fuel prices remained remarkably stable between 1921 and 1929. The prosperity of the tertiary sector is reflected in the rise in the prices included in the 'miscellaneous' column, mainly personal services.

It is perhaps surprising, in the light of what has been said about agriculture, to find that average food prices did rise in the 1920s (though by a mere 9 per cent in eight years, as much as we have become accustomed to accept in as many months in recent times). Different foods behaved very differently : the main increase was indubitably for meat of all kinds; coffee, bread and milk also rose slightly in price; among the items for which urban consumers paid less and less as the decade proceeded were sugar, margarine and many vegetables. The price of butter was the same in 1929 as in 1923. To some extent, of course, the indexes of food prices do not compare like with like. One feature of the decade was that the processing and packaging industries were adding more to the value (and cost) of food before it reached the market. The final product was economically, if not always gastronomically, more advanced.

We may conclude with the following observations :

(i) The 1920s present a fairly unusual picture of prosperity and full employment (by post-1945 standards) without inflation.

(ii) The general appearance of price stability conceals variations between years and among commodities.

(iii) At the same time, the question has to be asked whether, given the improvements in productivity, price stability was enough. This steadiness has in fact been regarded by some as a 'concealed inflation'. Should not prices have been falling (or falling faster) to pass on the productivity gains to the consumer?

(iv) At this stage, one has to turn away from the 'real' factors in the economy to the 'policy' factors, i.e. monetary policy, will be discussed in a later part of this chapter (pp. 83–5).

2 Institutions

(a) *Banks.* Although American industries had consolidated them-selves, much more than their British counterparts, into a few large corporations, American banking, in contrast with the British 'Big Five', remained highly decentralised in many small units. As seen earlier, there were in the 1920s some 30,000 separate, unitary banks. Most of these were single-office institutions, entirely dependent upon their own resources. If people who had deposited their savings in a bank began to get anxious and withdrew their money, a run on the bank could quickly develop. Being on its own, the bank could not turn to any other institution for help. Anxiety quickly led to panic and panic led rapidly to a bank closure. Thus the atomistic structure of American banking was an element of weakness, especially since the smallest banks were usually in the countryside. Hence the *economic* weakness of agriculture was aggravated by the *institutional* weakness of the banking system.

Since the 1830s there had been no central bank in the United States, no American equivalent of the Bank of England. The Federal Reserve Act of 1913 had attempted to provide some kind of central control of banking, but stopped far short of establishing a single central bank. But the Federal Reserve System was still in its infancy in the 1920s; its policies between the mid-1920s and 1933 will be discussed on pp. 83–5. In many important respects, however, the Federal Reserve System had to await the reforms introduced under the New Deal before it became fully operational.

(b) *Industrial corporations.* American industry had assumed its twentieth-century corporate structure around the turn of the century, and in most industries a peak of monopolisation was reached soon after 1900. It was pointed out earlier (pp. 23–4, 40–1) that the experience of wartime collaboration among businessmen, together with the Supreme Court's decision of 1920 not to order the dissolution of the U.S. Steel Corporation, meant that there was no return in the 1920s to the anti-trust crusading zeal of the 1900s. Mainly because of the development of new firms, the degree of monopolisation probably did not increase in the decade; but it did not diminish either. Rather there emerged a situation of oligopoly in the structure of American industry.

It is very likely that this oligopolistic structure was one of the reasons why, in certain sectors at least, prices were not reduced as far as the improvements in productivity might have permitted. The price rigidities were, in other words, attributable in part to the nature of corporate institutions in this decade.[15]

(c) *The Federal Trade Commission.* This body had been established by the Clayton Act and been given the task of enforcing the codes embodied in the Act. As with the Federal Reserve System, the F.T.C. still lacked teeth, and perhaps also will-power, in its role as national watch-dog against price-fixing and other acts of 'collusion in restraint of trade'.

(*d*) *Trade unions.* With the demise of the Industrial Workers of the World (I.W.W.), the American Federation of Labor (A.F. of L.) was left alone in the field. Its policy was to restrict membership to skilled workers. The unskilled – the poorest paid – were still completely unorganised in unions in the 1920s. Even the member unions of the A.F. of L. were weak in the 1920s and total membership declined from 5 million to 3½ million. The weakness of American trade unions in this decade is paradoxical. Normally unions are expected to gain strength during a period of prosperity when labour is in demand. Two factors here might be noted : the development in some industries of what was called 'welfare capitalism' including the establishment of Company Unions; and the fact already noted that industrial employment did not expand as rapidly as the industrial production figures might suggest.

As seen earlier, industrial real wages grew by about 45 per cent, the main improvement occurring before 1925. It is also evident that the main gains went to the skilled section of the work force.

Although it may well be true that in the long run trade union activities have not, in the United States or in Britain, significantly increased the share of total incomes accruing to the working class,* it may nevertheless also be true that in the short run they have had some influence. It is at least arguable that the weakness of American trade unions was a causal factor of the economic imbalance in the distribution of incomes discussed earlier. In simple terms, there was nothing in the structure of American trade unions in this decade to jolt the economy into the needed redistribution of the productivity gains. Thus, just as corporation strength operated in the direction of resisting price reductions, union weakness did not create pressures to raise still further the already considerable wage increases.

(*e*) *The stock market.* The most patent sign of disturbance in the American economy from the mid-1920s on was the mounting fever of speculation on the New York Stock Exchange. The detailed story of the Wall Street panic and collapse in October 1929 has been told in many places[16] and will only be reviewed here in outline.

The market value of shares listed on the New York Stock Ex-

---

* As asserted for instance by the economist Thomas Balogh (Lord Balogh) in a letter to *The Times* (8 September 1969): 'For almost 25 years the unions tried to use their industrial power to obtain a higher share for wages in the national income. Despite the vast reinforcement of their bargaining strength by full employment they were wholly unsuccessful.'

change rose from $4 billion in 1923 to $67 billion at the beginning of 1929. The rise in the index of monthly average stock prices (based on 421 common stocks; 1926 = 100) accelerated to 130 by the end of 1927, 150 early in 1928, neared 180 by the end of that year and had reached almost 230 at the peak in September 1929. During those first nine months of 1929, a further $20 billion was added to share values, the total reaching about $90 billion by the end of September. The runaway inflation of stock prices was helped by the willingness of some New York brokers to advance loans for Stock Exchange speculation on a 25 per cent cash deposit and by the growth of legitimate investment trusts as well as purely speculative pools. Some attempts were made to check these activities, particularly by certain banks which reduced their loans to brokers, but the continuing influx of new money into the money market nullified these efforts. In the early months of 1929 the Federal Reserve Board, among others, warned of the dangers inherent in the mounting speculation and prevailed on brokers to raise the cash deposit requirement to 50 per cent.

Speculation continued to mount, however, until September 1929. By that time the market began to show signs of alarm and some prices began to level out, others to fall; by the end of the month the losses exceeded the gains and the peak of expansion appeared to have been passed. In the early days of October selling continued and prices fell still further, but then something like erratic stabilisation appeared to set in. At this stage optimistic pronouncements were made proclaiming that a lower, safer plateau had been reached from which a general recovery might proceed; indeed some observers (including Keynes in England) positively welcomed the decline as the needed corrective to unsound speculation which would release funds for real industrial investment.

The final landslide occurred in two separate avalanches: on 23 and 24 October and on 28 and 29 October. The number of shares sold on those four dates tell their own story: over 6 million and almost 13 million respectively on the first two days; desperate attempts over the intervening weekend to shore up the market were of no avail and the crash continued with 9 million shares sold on the 28th and finally 16.4 million on the day of ultimate despair, Black Tuesday, 29 October 1929.

By December total share values had fallen from the peak of $90 billion in September to about $65 billion, the level of January 1929, and the index of common stock prices had fallen by about 40 per cent to its mid-1928 level. For the individuals concerned these falls involved immense losses but it is still arguable that, as some contemporary economists maintained, they had merely cancelled out the unsound speculation of early and mid-1929 and restored the market to the sounder 1928 situation. Indeed, the early months of 1930 saw a decided recovery of stock prices; but from the spring of 1930 to the summer of 1932 there was an almost unbroken decline; the price index quoted earlier (1926 = 100) had fallen from its peak of almost 230 in September 1929 to 150 by the end of the year; it reached 100 early in 1931 and a year later was below 50, its level for several months of 1932.

At this stage we are mainly concerned with the weaknesses in the structure of existing American institutions, not with the connection between the Wall Street slump and the subsequent general economic depression. It will have become clear from the above brief narrative of events that (a) negatively, there were neither automatic nor manipulative brakes to halt either the speculative mania of 1929 or the subsequent precipitate decline; and (b) positively, institutional devices, such as stock trading on the margin, actually facilitated the speculation. To the inadequacy of institutions and their practices there has also to be added the deficiencies of the available personnel; partly because of America's changed role in the world, and partly because of Wall Street's enlarged functions, the human expertise required to handle the business of Wall Street was as inadequate as the institutions.

But both in rise and in fall, the events on Wall Street had their basis in human psychology, indicated by the use of the words 'mania' for the speculative phase and 'depression' for the decline. Once all hopes of profitability appeared to have vanished, then the task of bringing about recovery was inextricably linked with the near-impossible task of persuading potential investors, in any case a diminishing breed, that investment could once again be worth while.

3 Government policies

Given the above economic and institutional circumstances, what government policies were pursued in the 1920s, and how far did they alleviate or aggravate the problems that existed? Clearly no major *institutional* reforms were undertaken during the decade;

such measures would have been very far from the thinking and the personality of both Harding and Coolidge. Nevertheless other steps, including the rejection of certain proposals, must have influenced the economic climate, if only negatively.

An important problem faces us at once. It was stressed earlier that the United States had emerged from the First World War with the strongest economy in the world and as the world's leading creditor nation. She had in some degree moved into the position Britain had held in the second half of the nineteenth century. But there was an important difference. Whereas Britain's own internal economic interest and that of most parts of the developing international economy generally coincided, this was not necessarily so in America's foreign economic relations. The United States always had been, and could continue to be, far more economically self-sufficient than Britain ever was. Crudely stated this meant that while the rest of the world now depended on the United States in many different ways, the United States did not depend on the rest of the world to anything like the same extent. To take the most obvious illustration of this point, while Britain's imports for many decades regularly amounted to between 25 per cent and 30 per cent of her national income, America's imports were under 5 per cent of hers. Yet to the countries supplying those imports to the United States, the goods they exported to America might be crucial to their whole balance of trade. Similarly, America's export of capital was a small fraction of her total investment but was often of significant proportions to the countries receiving that capital. In either case to curtail imports or to cut down (or withdraw) foreign capital investment might be of relatively little significance to America but of enormous consequence to all, or some of, the countries affected.

Given the disturbed conditions of international economic life after 1918, America's policies were critical to the outside world; disequilibrium arose out of war destruction, movement of the terms of trade against primary producers, war debts and reparations, and the creation of new nation states.

America's changed position in the world economy thus created new and difficult conflicts of policy. Could she continue to operate as if in isolation and ignore the effects her domestic measures might produce elsewhere? Was it now short-sighted to suppose that an affluent America could exist in a disturbed world? Was the assumption still correct that America's own prosperity was largely unaffected by conditions outside?

The pre-war international economy had been based on the free flow of productive resources and of end-products; on Britain's willingness to export capital and import goods; on America's willingness (and that of some other countries) to allow labour to move by migration to its area of greatest profitability; and on the working of the Gold Standard in so far as it maintained stable exchange rates through the mechanism of internal inflations and deflations where needed. In the 1920s, however, the United States (i) stopped the unrestricted entry of labour into her economy; (ii) re-introduced a high tariff (in contrast with Britain's former, and still continuing, free-trade policy); (iii) did not allow the inflow of gold to inflate her prices and so restore the balance of trade. In other words, it is often argued that the United States in the 1920s refused to accept the responsibilities of having become the world's major economy, but continued in her policies as if nothing had changed since before 1914 (which was indeed what the 'return to normalcy' implied).

The validity of this argument may be assessed by a brief examination in turn of American policies in the 1920s.

(a) *Immigration restriction: the Quota Acts of 1921 and 1924.* For three hundred years, America (first the colonies and then the United States) had willingly accepted immigrants from all parts of the world, an attitude symbolised in the welcoming torch of the Statue of Liberty in New York harbour. In the century before 1920, some 34 million immigrants had arrived in America, over eight times more immigrants than the number of Americans when the United States became a nation in 1790, or about as many as the entire population of the United Kingdom at the end of the nineteenth century. If imported goods contributed a mere 5 per cent of America's national income, imported people accounted for over 40 per cent of America's population growth in the three decades 1890 to 1920. In the ten years 1905–14 over 10 million foreigners entered the United States, an average of over 1 million per year or over 84,000 per month, nearly 20,000 per week, or over 2700 persons *per day*. By 1920 there was a widespread feeling that this had gone on long enough.

An Act of 1882 had excluded convicts, lunatics and other categories deemed undesirable and one of 1917 enumerated thirty categories subject to exclusion and imposed a test of literacy. But neither Act involved any general limitation of numbers, or exclusion by country of origin (the only exceptions to this being the limitation of oriental immigration by the Chinese Exclusion Act of 1882 and the 'Gentlemen's Agreement 'with Japan of 1908).

The first law embodying such quantitative restrictions was the Emergency Quota Act of 1921, passed under war emergency provisions and extended, as a temporary measure, until 1924. Total admissions were limited to a maximum of 357,000 per year (about the same as the average of 364,000 per year in the decade 1893–1902 but far below the immediate pre-war average of one million) and a 'quota' was established of 3 per cent of the foreign-born of each nationality resident in the United States in the most recent Census (that of 1910, as the 1920 figures were not yet available). The basis of 'foreign-born residents' gave an advantage to the 'new' immigrants from Southern and Eastern Europe who had constituted the bulk of immigration in the two or three decades before 1910.

The Quota Act of 1924 was much more restrictive, drastically lowering the annual maximum to 160,000. More significantly it changed the basis of the quota calculation from the 'foreign-born resident' qualification to one of 'national origins'; i.e. the new calculation would include an attempt to assess the origins of all native-born Americans as well as the foreign-born. As an interim measure (until final quotas were worked out, eventually in 1929) the quota would be 2 per cent of the foreign-born in the United States in 1890. Both the interim quotas, which operated from 1924 to 1929, and the eventual quotas calculated on the 'national origins' principle, greatly increased the allocation to countries of Western Europe, and especially to Britain, and severely curtailed the numbers admissible from 'new immigration' countries.

Partly as a result of these measures, immigration into the United States fell in the course of the 1920s from over 650,000 Europeans in 1921 (before the first Quota Act) to an annual average of just under the quota figure of 160,000 between 1925 and 1929; in 1921, 222,000 Italians arrived, for example, but after 1925 the number never exceeded 22,000. After 1930 America no longer offered any attraction and immigration was reduced to a trickle (indeed, allowing for those who returned to their homes, there probably was a net emigration during the depression years).

The effects of America's immigration policy closed the long-open door to emigration as a solution to problems of unemployment in European countries. What concerns us here is the effect on the American economy. The curtailment of immigration certainly emphasised the declining trend of American population growth (see above, pp. 30–1) which fell in the 1930s to below 10 per cent, the lowest ever, and also the retardation in urban growth. The restriction particularly affected the productive age group between twenty and thirty years since that had always been the predominant age of immigrants. The importance of the declining rate of population growth will be discussed later as it formed one of the major items in the 'stagnation thesis' of Professor Alvin Hansen (see below, pp. 104–7).

(b) *Tariff policy*. The argument in favour of a protective tariff had been stated by Alexander Hamilton, the first Secretary of the Treasury, in his *Report on the Subject of Manufacturers* of 1791. In order to further the growth of America's infant industries, Hamilton argued, it was necessary to shelter them from the competition of more advanced European imports by taxing those goods as they entered the country. For the first half-century of America's national history the debate swayed back and forth and was one element in the North–South cleavage which culminated in the Civil War. At the time of the Civil War, America entered on full-blooded protection, even though it was already beginning to be evident that many of her industries were beyond the stage of infancy.

Between the Civil War and the First World War the average rate of tariff was high enough to prevent effective competition from imports for many areas of manufacturing. During the period of protection industry expanded rapidly and many were prone to the special pleading, *post hoc ergo propter hoc*; growth and prosperity were due to the tariff. What is surprising is the weakness of the opposition, but support for Protection was as emotional an act of faith as the belief in Free Trade in Britain.

It was not until Woodrow Wilson's election to the presidency in 1912 that any major reduction was made in the tariff. The Underwood–Simmons Tariff Act of 1913 restored the average level of tariffs roughly to the 1860, pre-Civil War level, increased the number of items on the free-trade list. Earlier in the same year the Sixteenth Amendment to the Constitution had made possible the introduction of a federal income tax.

The effects of the 1913 tariff reduction were blunted by the First World War which provided far more effective protection than any tariff. Once the war was over there was no better indication of the meaning of Harding's 'normalcy' than the Emergency Tariff Act of 1921, confirmed in the Fordney–McCumber Tariff of 1922. It has traditionally been maintained that by keeping imports out by means of this high tariff the United States aggravated the existing imbalances in the world economy. A more recent view,[17] persuasively argued, has suggested that the effects of Fordney–McCumber were psychological and symbolic rather than real. A lower American tariff would have made little difference. Given her self-sufficiency, what indeed might the United States have bought at a competitive price from the outside world? The main items which America wanted to import – coffee, raw silk, natural rubber, copper, paper, and some tropical fruits – were either exempt from the tariff or were subject to a low duty. Imports from Europe consisted largely of specialised, high-quality goods which supplemented rather than competed with American products.

It is probable, then, that in practice the Fordney–McCumber Tariff made little difference. But symbols can be as important in determining behaviour as actualities. If industrialists believed that the tariff rendered them immune from foreign competition, then their resistance to price reductions was correspondingly increased. And if, to the outside world, the tariff seemed to proclaim that Uncle Sam was not interested in the economic problems of other countries, then one more disturbing factor was unnecessarily present in the extremely delicate international economic situation.

(c) *Fiscal policy.* It almost goes without saying that the federal government made no conscious attempt to use the budget as a means of regulating the national economy. Nevertheless, no budget can be neutral, even though its consequences are unintentional. Andrew W. Mellon was appointed Secretary of the Treasury by Harding and remained in that office until 1932 when Hoover appointed him Ambassador to Great Britain. His main policy was tax reduction and in this he certainly succeeded.

Total federal expenditure and income both remained virtually unchanged in every year from 1922 to 1929. If the aim was a balanced budget, then revenue was always underestimated since receipts always exceeded expenditure; the total surplus amounted to $6.8 billion and the gross national debt was reduced by about $6 billion.

TABLE 19

Federal Government finances, 1923–9

Year	Receipts in billions of dollars	Expenditure in billions of dollars	Surplus in billions of dollars
1923	4.0	3.3	0.7
1924	4.0	3.0	1.0
1925	3.8	3.1	0.7
1926	4.0	3.1	0.9
1927	4.1	3.0	1.2
1928	4.0	3.1	0.9
1929	4.0	3.3	0.7

SOURCE: *Historical Statistics of the United States*, p. 711.

The net impact of these fiscal operations must have been mildly deflationary. Purchasing power was withdrawn from the public to the amount of the revenue surplus and the public debt was retired without any increase in public spending (though it is true that the debt repayments in effect returned those sums to the economy, for private spending or saving).

The extraordinary stability of the aggregate figures for government finance conceals an increase in the yield from certain items, notably customs duties and income-tax.

A crucial policy decision was taken in the budget of 1927. With a surplus of almost 1 billion dollars in 1926 (and reaching $1.15 billion in 1927) the opportunity was taken to lower the income-tax (for details, see below, p. 145). In retrospect this can be adjudged a mistake, particularly in the light of later Keynesian economics. The benefits of the lower tax rates accrued to the wealthiest classes thus adding to the propensity to over-saving and feeding fuel to the Stock Exchange speculation of 1928–9. Still more significantly, however, the opportunity was not taken to increase government expenditure even though signs were already beginning to appear that expansion was slowing down in important sectors of the economy.

The argument is not that fiscal policy was a crucial factor of maladjustment in the 1920s, but rather that it was just one more pressure in the wrong direction, all pushing the distribution of resources towards less spending and more saving. It would be a nice theoretical exercise to estimate what adjustments to fiscal policy, and in what year, would have been appropriate to rectify the drift of the economy.

(d) *Monetary policy.* More attention has been paid to monetary policy in the 1920s than to any other area of economic control during the period. As seen earlier the decade may be regarded as a unique example of prosperity combined with price stability, expansion without inflation. At the same time it is sometimes argued that since costs of production were falling sharply as a result of increased efficiency prices should also have been falling much more than they did, so that there was in fact a concealed inflation. Seen from an international point of view, however, the American monetary system in the 1920s was accused of the opposite : America's surplus of exports over imports, together with her insistence on debt repayment, resulted in a net gold import of almost $1\frac{1}{2}$ billion between 1920 and 1929, augmented by domestic production. Yet between 1922 and 1929 the internal money supply increased by only 20 per cent (though admittedly with a higher velocity of circulation), while the gross national product increased by double that amount. It can hardly be argued that the economic expansion was artificially fed by an excessive expansion of the money supply. Contemporaries indeed complained that the United States did not 'play the game' according to the 'rules of the Gold Standard'; the gold was sterilised in Fort Knox. Equilibrium in the international economy required American prices to rise in order to reduce her exports; some have argued that Britain's return to the Gold Standard in 1925 was based on the expectation that American prices would shortly have to rise.

These interpretations all attribute to American monetary authority a greater sense of purpose than in fact existed. The Federal Reserve System had been created as recently as 1914. It did not vest control in one single, central bank on the model of the Bank of

England. Gradually leadership devolved upon the Governors of the twelve Federal Reserve Banks. The Governor of the New York Reserve Bank in the 1920s was Benjamin Strong and most writers have regarded Strong as the dominating figure in American monetary policy until his death in 1928, more or less the American eqivalent of Montagu Norman in Britain.

The orthodox interpretation is that the Federal Reserve System, under the purposeful guidance of Benjamin Strong, was successful at least until 1927 both in setting up appropriate ends and in devising suitable means to achieve them. The primary object was price stability and the main instrumentality was the development of techniques and an administrative apparatus of open-market operations. Other incidental benefits accrued : incipient recessions in 1924 and 1927 were halted; the international measures to restore the Gold Standard in 1925 were supported, but international considerations were always secondary to domestic ones. With Strong's hand removed in 1928, the argument continues, monetary policy moved sharply from success to failure : the efforts by monetary authorities to stem first the Stock Exchange speculation and then its collapse in 1929 failed abysmally; in 1931 the tight money policy was disastrous; in 1932 the widespread closures of banks all over the country could and should have been halted by suitable measures.

Professor E. R. Wicker has challenged this interpretation in almost every particular.[18] The Federal Reserve Board did not have a clear aim of achieving price stability in the 1920s. If prices did remain relatively stable it was not due to deliberate manipulation by the monetary authorities. The Board was in fact, in his view, prepared to allow increases in the money supply and in bank credit if the result would be to give a boost to production and even if higher prices resulted. Similarly Governor Strong, in Wicker's opinion, was much more influenced by international considerations than the normal view allows, and even exhibited a 'nostalgia for the so-called rules of the Gold Standard game', i.e. the most effective stabiliser was not the management of the domestic currency but the traditional international monetary framework and automatic mechanisms.

It is probably reasonable to suggest that the *ex post* record of price stability has led to a rationalisation of the activities of the Federal Reserve System and the conclusion that its actions facilitated or even caused that outcome. It is probably doubtful that banking theory and techniques were sufficiently developed and understood, by the practitioners at least, in the 1920s to permit a positive and successful policy.

Over the alleged failures of monetary policy towards the end of the decade there can be less argument. Here, however, the fault may have lain rather in institutional inadequacies than in policy errors. The monetary governors may have had the desire, but did not have the determination, the authority or the instruments, to halt the use of bank credit for speculation in 1929 or the widespread bank failures of the subsequent years.

(e) *Agricultural policy*. The reasons why, despite the slight rise in food prices, many farmers did not share the general prosperity of the decade have been discussed earlier. From the moment the first signs of distress appeared with the fall in farm prices and incomes late in 1920, the cry began to be heard, 'Do something for the farmer'. The farm interest was well represented in Congress and in May 1921 a 'farm bloc' came into existence, including some 20 Senators and 100 Representatives. This powerful pressure group was inter-regional and cross-party, uniting the cotton South and the corn Mid-west, progressives like George W. Norris (Nebraska) and Robert La Follette (Wisconsin) with conservatives like 'Cotton Ed' Smith (S. Carolina) and Arthur Capper (Kansas). A National Agriculture Conference was called in 1922 by the Secretary of Agriculture, Henry C. Wallace (not to be confused with F. D. Roosevelt's Secretary of Agriculture, Henry A. Wallace). Many proposals for the relief of farm distress were made and much was heard of 'justice' and 'fair shares'. The importance of the conference was that its final report put forward for the first time the notion of parity prices for agriculture, using the period 1910–14 as the bench-mark for comparison.

The main positive proposals emerging during the 1920s were those incorporated in the so-called McNary–Haugen legislation. The bill, supported by the American Farm Bureau Federation (formed in 1920), came four times before Congress. It was defeated in the House in 1924 and in both houses in 1926, but passed Congress in 1927 and 1928 only to be vetoed on both occasions by President Coolidge. The bill was a mixed package : high tariffs should be imposed on all imported agricultural commodities; a two-tier price system would be established whereby sales in home markets would be maintained by a specially constituted corporation at a 'fair exchange value', while sales to foreign markets would be allowed to follow world prices (assumed to be lower than the supported internal price); the price-support arrangements would be financed out of an 'equalisation fee' paid by participating farmers on every bale of cotton or bushel of wheat sold to the corporation. The arithmetic of the proposal was that the farmer would gain the difference between the supported price and the free-market price, minus his fee to the corporation.

Although most writers have regarded the non-adoption of the McNary–Haugen proposals as a characteristic example of the *laissez-faire* attitudes of the 1920s, it is by no means certain that they would have provided any solution to the agricultural problem either in the short- or in the long-term.[19] The proposals contained no suggestions for dealing with the surplus products of agriculture (beyond foreign dumping) yet tried to guarantee a profitable price to farmers no matter how much they produced. The main beneficiaries would have been the fairly select group of single-crop farmers who produced especially for export markets – the wheat, cotton and tobacco producers. Those farmers who were already diversifying their production to meet domestic demand – dairy farmers, fruit-growers, stock-raisers, vegetable producers and mixed farmers generally – were not enthusiastic about McNary–Haugen.

The proposals, moreover, contained no solution for the problem of farm debt. Loans had been raised by farmers for purposes of expansion in the days of high prices and immediately after the war. Interest now had to be paid on those loans, and if possible the capital repaid, in circumstances of reduced incomes – a recurring problem throughout American history but no nearer solution in 1926 than in 1786.

We can certainly conclude that the Federal Government did nothing 'to help the farmer' before Hoover's Agricultural Marketing Act of 1929 (see p. 97), and it can probably be said that the McNary–Haugen proposals, if implemented, would have been unlikely to solve any of the basic problems, though they would have helped certain groups of farmers almost literally at the expense of the rest. It had not yet been understood that the quickest way to 'help the farmer' economically was to make the secondary and tertiary sectors of the economy even stronger, in order to improve market conditions and provide even more alternative job opportunities for farmers and their families.

(*f*) *Transport.* The 1920s saw the ground prepared for what in the 1930s was to become an important area of government intervention : road building, encouragement of civil aviation, and help for the railroads.

Following the first step in the Federal Aid Road Act of 1916, the Federal Highway Act of 1921 set the stage for the road-building boom of the 1920s. Between 1922 and 1929 80,000 miles of federally-assisted road were completed at a cost of $670 million to the federal government and $869 million to the state governments. In the light of the earlier discussion of fiscal policy, it might be noted, however, that federal expenditure in this field was at its peak in 1925 and fell in each successive year until 1929; mileage completed also declined after 1925. Here, therefore, we have direct evidence of the failure to expand federal activity and expenditure. It might also be noted that this was one area of expansion under Hoover : federal expenditure on roads grew from $80 million in 1929 to over $220 million in 1931 with a corresponding increase in mileage completed.

Air travel was still in its infancy but the Post Office began to establish an air-mail service in the early 1920s and the Air Commerce Act passed in 1926 was the ground law for subsequent federal assistance and control. At this stage the main activity was in the establishment of radio navigational aids.

The rise of the motor-car quickly led to the first signs of the decline of the railroads. Although revenue from freight traffic slightly increased during the commercially active years of the 1920s, passenger traffic began to decline and the mileage of railway line abandoned exceeded new construction. The return of the railroads to private ownership in the Transportation Act of 1920 was a landmark in policy-making in that attention shifted thereafter from the former goal of protecting the public to the new one of reconciling protection of the railroads with the 'public interest'. The old Interstate Commerce Commission, originally set up in 1887 for quite different purposes, was retained as the main instrument of policy and its powers were very considerably increased. What still remained unresolved was where exactly the 'public interest' lay and how the many conflicting interpretations of that 'interest', for example the sharply divergent 'interests' of different regions, were to be reconciled.

4 Summary and conclusion

An attempt must now be made to answer, or at any rate to re-formulate the question with which this section began on p. 59. Was the depression which gradually engulfed the American economy after 1929 a direct consequence of developments occurring during the prosperity of the 1920s? Implicit in the foregoing survey of economic conditions, institutions and policies in the twenties has been an indication that there were at least partial, direct causal connections. Clearly an analysis of American economic life in the 1920s does reveal weaknesses, above all in the imbalance between the different sectors of the economy, which, when aggravated, led to dire consequences. American institutions, having evolved over the previous century and a half, were patently inadequate to meet the stresses and strains of the new patterns and demands of a rapidly changing economy. Of course many wrong policies were pursued, or perhaps it would be more accurate to say that more appropriate policies were not pursued. The most obvious direct causal connections occurred in an area where economic weakness, institutional inadequacy and faulty policy all met, the great acceleration in the speed of the Wall Street inflation culminating in the great crash at the end of 1929.

These admissions, however, stop far short of the view that the eventual deep depression of 1932–3, to which the Wall Street crash was only the prelude, was in any way an *inevitable* consequence of the prosperity of the twenties. The foregoing survey implicitly assumed that the economic problems of the 1920s, though serious, were not insurmountable; that the institutions, though often anachronistic, were not wholly devoid of merit; that the policies, or lack of policies, caused irritants to conditions they did nothing to improve, but that they did not create those conditions. The economy, however, had none of the built-in stabilisers of today. Many of the institutions while serving their purpose adequately when no strains were present were fragile under the hammer. Consequently a conjuncture of circumstances meant that, once the decisive movement towards calamity had occurred, a gathering momentum built up which was difficult to arrest.

The first problem is to identify more carefully the timing of that decisive movement. It is convenient but unsatisfactory to date it from the Wall Street crash. As seen earlier, the expansion of the

1920s was not a regular, year-by-year improvement. Many observers have seen the beginning of the depression in the retardation of growth which became visible in some sectors as early as 1925. On the other hand it will be suggested later (pp. 92–3) that it was not until the middle of 1931 that the decisive down-turn occurred, nearly two years after the Wall Street crash.

The second problem relates to the severity of the eventual depression. The question to be answered is not so much why the Stock Market collapsed or even why the economy went into decline, but why the depression turned out to be so severe and so protracted and why it was worse in the United States than anywhere else in the world. Before we proceed to examine some of the answers which economists have given to these questions, it is appropriate to summarise the events of 1929 to 1933.

It is important to remind ourselves, however, of the character of the nation that confronted these events. The America of the late 1920s was very different from that of 1910 but, just as in Britain, outlook and attitudes changed far more slowly than economic and social conditions. Farmers, industrialists, investors, professional men (and women), retailers, trade union leaders and politicians all retained many assumptions in their behaviour that were no longer valid and that were in many respects dangerous. Many of these attitudes, for example, conspired unwittingly together with the institutions and the policies to restrain that redistribution of the gains of higher productivity which the situation required. To repeat an earlier proposition, the problems of a world of twentieth-century technology were being met with a nineteenth-century ideology.

Let us allow Calvin Coolidge to have the last word on the decade over which he presided.

Men do not make laws. They discover them. . . . The weaknesses of representative government is the weakness of us imperfect human beings who administer it. . . . Do the day's work. If it be to protect the rights of the weak, whoever objects, do it. . . . Don't hesitate to be as revolutionary as science. Don't hesitate to be as reactionary as the multiplication table. Don't expect to build up the weak by pulling down the strong.

All admirable old precepts. But all negative precisely at the time when new positive philosophies were urgently required.

4

Depression 1929–33

I HERBERT HOOVER

The years of economic crisis which followed the Wall Street collapse of 1929 coincided almost exactly and have commonly been identified with the period of office of the Republican President, Herbert Hoover. In the subsequent election of 1932 Hoover was decisively rejected, the only twentieth-century American President (apart from Taft in 1912) to be removed from the White House in a presidential election. Yet Hoover's majority of 6.4 million over Al Smith in 1928 was only fractionally less than the majority of 7 million by which he was in turn defeated by F. D. Roosevelt in 1932. In other words, he entered the White House with a large popular following, a splendid record of public service behind him and a vast fund of confidence and goodwill on which to draw.

Born in mid-western Iowa but brought up on the west coast in Oregon, Hoover had been in turn mechanical engineer, geologist and mining consultant, the latter in many parts of the world. In 1917 he had become the head of the U.S. Food Administration and later of the American Relief Association; in January 1920 head of the European Relief Council. He appeared to be that new twentieth-century figure, the cosmopolitan technologist. Nor was he actively partisan: in 1920 his name was canvassed as a possible *Democratic* candidate for the presidency, with Franklin D. Roosevelt as his running-mate, to oppose the Republican team of Harding–Coolidge.

In the euphoria of late-1920s prosperity, the economic situation was not seriously at issue in the 1928 campaign. Only two matters counted: Prohibition (Drys, Hoover, versus Wets, Smith); and religion, since Al Smith was a Roman Catholic. (The very embodiment of the American Melting Pot, with Irish, English, Italian and German grandparents, he was also – with his Lower East Side upbringing – almost the only presidential candidate to emerge from a wholly metropolitan background.) Al Smith secured a majority in all the twelve largest cities but his Wetness and Catholicism lost him the normal Democratic allegiance of many Southern states.

Prophets of doom are rarely castigated if their dire forebodings do not eventuate, partly perhaps because their warnings may have helped avoid the misfortunes they predicted. But a note of false optimism, once sounded, has a habit of reverberating to infinity. Herbert Hoover had the misfortune to articulate in 1928 what the vast majority of Americans believed, that a brave new world was on the brink of realisation. Looking back on the vast improvements of the immediately preceding years he ventured to say during the election campaign of 1928 : 'We in America are nearer to the final triumph over poverty than ever before in the history of any land. . . . We shall soon, with the help of God, be in sight of the day when poverty shall be banished from the nation.' In the gathering gloom and mounting distress of the depression after 1929 these hollow words were neither forgotten nor forgiven. When, a year after the Wall Street crash, Hoover still continued to make optimistic pronouncements he was patently hoping that a prediction of prosperity would be self-fulfilling.

Hoover came to the White House well experienced in government administration. As Secretary of Commerce under Harding in 1921, he had seen the economy pass through an economic depression. It is easy in retrospect to regard the Great Depression as inevitable and to castigate those who did not see it coming. Yet conditions in 1921 were in many respects worse than in 1930 (1921, average unemployment 5 million, or 12 per cent; 1930, 4 million or 9 per cent), but on that occasion the economy had rapidly recovered.

The main precedent to which Hoover therefore turned for guidance was one in which the economy had righted itself and one which preceded a period of growth and prosperity. In 1930 at least these were still no clear indication that the economy would not again follow a similar course.

Hoover's initial response in 1929–30 was very similar to Harding's response in 1921 : call a conference. Hoover was no less an idealist than any other American in the 1920s.* He rested his faith in the

* Although Herbert Hoover has generally been denigrated by historians, he has a great supporter in the left-wing writer William Appleman Williams, in *The Contours of American History* (1961) pp. 425 ff., who regards him as badly misunderstood and misrepresented. A progressive of the 1900s, Hoover had helped Herbert Croly to start the publication *New Republic* in 1914 and was a close adviser of Woodrow Wilson after 1916. Franklin Roosevelt said of him in 1920: 'He is certainly a wonder, and I wish we could make him President of the United States.'

acceptance of social responsibility by industrial leaders; equally he believed that to increase the power of government until it became the dominant element in the nation was to start out on a very dangerous road indeed – especially if leadership rested with self-seeking politicians, or those representing narrow interest-groups.

Hoover took his distrust of congressional politicians to great lengths by insisting that the depression was to be treated as a natural disaster and therefore to be handled by the Executive and not by the corrupt demagogues on Capitol Hill. It was absurd to suppose, he held, 'that we can legislate ourselves out of a world-wide depression any more than we can exorcise a Caribbean hurricane by statutory law'. Executive action, not legislation was needed.

II THE FIRST PHASE OF THE DEPRESSION

Immediately after the stock market crash Hoover called a series of conferences of leading American businessmen at the White House in November 1929.[1] It was in accordance with his doctrine of responsible leadership that at each meeting Hoover secured a pledge from those present that, instead of cutting wages and laying off workers as in 1921, they would maintain wage levels, share out the available work and go ahead with construction projects already planned. In other words, Hoover committed himself to the view that the main responsibility for economic recovery fell on the business community.

Bankers appear to have been less willing than industrialists to support such positive action, taking the view (at least before the slide had gained momentum) that the recession should be allowed to run its course to provide the periodic pruning of unhealthy growth, dead wood and suckers that an economy needs. Nevertheless the Federal Reserve System used open-market operations from October 1929 to the end of 1930 to pump into the economy over half a million dollars of extra money (equivalent to $6 billion additional bank credit) and also reduced interest rates.

These two sets of measures – wage maintenance and easy money – appeared to work. Despite the demoralisation of Wall Street, the economy levelled out in the course of 1930 and there was every indication of definite stabilisation at a lower level. Industrial production fell but the decline halted at a lower plateau; durable-goods production in some sectors even began to expand; by December

1930 department-store sales were almost back to their January level and began to rise early in 1931. Although average unemployment in 1930 was almost 3 million higher than in 1929 it was still much below the 1921 level and at a rate only 1 per cent above that of 1922.

The real degeneration from economic recession into collapse has to be dated, not from the Wall Street crash of October 1929, but from the middle months of 1931 and considerable weight has to be attached to international events. The sterling crisis which began in April 1931 led to Britain's abandonment of the Gold Standard in September. As gold began to drain away from the United States, the Federal Reserve System reversed its easy money policy and tightened credit. The result was a new wave of selling on the Stock Exchange and a rush for liquidity. The latter led to runs on many banks and precipitated the wave of bank failures which reached its crest in the twelve-month period from March 1932 to March 1933 with over 4000 failures.

A further reversal occurred in October 1931 with the abandonment, first by the U.S. Steel Corporation but quickly by other businesses too, of the wage-maintenance agreements. This change of direction after two years of reasonable success had extremely adverse effects on every branch of the economy, extending beyond those sectors immediately affected. Unaccountably, given his principles, Hoover remained silent.

If the wage-maintenance agreements foreshadowed the later price-maintenance agreements embodied in Roosevelt's National Industrial Recovery Act (N.I.R.A.) (see pp. 120–1), an even closer parallel is found in the plan propounded in September 1931 by Gerard Swope, President of the General Electric Company. He proposed organising every branch of industry into trade associations, with a relaxation of the anti-trust laws to allow the exchange of information and the allocation of production quotas; in return industry would guarantee job security and provide unemployment insurance. The Swope Plan, a near blue-print for the N.R.A., was the most comprehensive plan to emerge during this period but did not secure Hoover's backing. He saw it as 'sheer fascism' and as 'the most gigantic proposal of monopoly ever made'.[2] As the N.R.A. was to prove, such steps were likely to lead to the domination of industry by the large firms. At this stage, it would appear, Hoover and the business community parted company. Contrary to the view depicted in most accounts Hoover had lost businessmen's confidence

93

and was regarded with as much distrust by them as by the rest of the community; he had failed to retain that confidence which had characterised the wage agreements of the first two years of his administration. Hoover was now alone in his preoccupation with the dangers of expanded government activity.

Meanwhile, members of Congress were not inactive. In the Senate in particular, Robert F. Wagner, Robert M. La Follette Jr., George W. Norris, Edward P. Costigan and others were the source of a constant flow of proposals, some embodied in bills, most of which either failed to pass Congress or were vetoed by Hoover.[3] If one is searching for antecedents to the New Deal, then it is here that they are to be found; the Senate, after all, has its own continuity which overlaps the presidential terms of office and a very real continuity of attitude and endeavour is to be found.

III THE COURSE OF THE DEPRESSION

The above narrative has suggested that the four years which followed the Wall Street crash did not see such an unbroken slide into disaster as has often been supposed and that, had it not been for international events and policy mistakes, there was a real chance of rectification for as long as two years afterwards. Those who prefer to view the period as one of uniform decline, however, would have little difficulty in mustering statistical evidence for their case.

Table 20 presents the catalogue of calamity. The most catastrophic decline was clearly in investment which, if calculated in constant dollars, fell to approximately one-tenth of its 1929 level by 1932 when it accounted for under 2 per cent of the sadly diminished G.N.P.; although the fall was severe enough in 1930, it was the later months of 1931 and the year 1932 that saw the most extreme curtailment of investment. Here was the crisis of confidence demonstrated in no uncertain fashion.

All the other data tell a similar story with varying degrees of severity (and those shown could be supplemented by countless others) : car sales and steel production down to one-quarter the 1929 level; farm receipts and incomes down by around one-half; employment down, and unemployment up, by 10 million; G.N.P. down by one-third.

We must not allow these cold statistics to conceal the human faces behind them. The resultant physical hardships were intense and

TABLE 20

Indicators of depression, 1929–33

G.N.P.	1929	1930	1931	1932	1933
Total ($ bill.)	104	91	76	59	56
Index at constant prices	100	90	83	71	69
Employment					
Av. at work (m.)	47.6	45.5	42.4	38.9	38.8
Av. unemployed (m.)	1.6	4.3	8.0	12.1	12.8
% unemployed	3.2	8.7	15.9	23.6	24.9
Investment					
Total ($ bill.)	16.2	10.3	5.5	0.9	1.4
as % G.N.P.	16	11	7	2	3
Industry					
Manufacturing Production Index (1929=100)	100	83	67	52	63
Total steel output (1929=100)*	100	72	46	24	41
Passenger car sales (m.)	4.5	2.8	1.9	1.1	1.6
Farming					
Cash receipts from farming ($ bill.)	11.3	9.1	6.4	4.8	5.5
Index of farm wage rates (1929=100)†	100	94	71	53	48

SOURCE: *Historical Statistics of the United States; Economic Reports of the President* (Indexes re-calculated).

* The 1930 level was about the same as the average output in 1922–5. The 1932 figure of 13.7 m. long tons was the lowest since 1900.

† In 1932 the Index of Composite Farm Wage Rates was approximately equal to the average for 1900–14.

affected millions of Americans. But more serious still was the demoralisation that affected people in all walks of life, from the bankrupt WASP businessman to the evicted black sharecropper. The supreme, sublime optimism of the later twenties turned slowly, sourly, into the helpless, hopeless despair of the thirties. The Jazzman had sung in the twenties : 'The more I get, the more I want it seems. . . .' His words now became : 'If you can't give a dollar, give me a lousy dime. . . .' The index that dropped furthest was the 'index of expectation' which fell all the way to zero and below. In the long run this was the worst calamity, since recovery depended on confidence and confidence in 1932–3 was non-existent.

When all the horror stories of the depression years have been told, however, the experiences have to be set in historical perspective. The years did not see famine and mass starvation; there was no 'mortality crisis' such as characterised periods of economic difficulty in previous centuries. The number of people dying did not increase dramatically. Indeed, despite a growing and an ageing population,* the number of deaths actually fell annually from 1929 to 1932. The death rate in 1932 and 1933 was the lowest ever, and both white and non-white population had a lower death rate in the 1930s than in the 1920s as Table 21 indicates. Even the causes of death confirm the general pattern; the main increases in the early 1930s occurred in deaths through suicide and motor vehicle accidents (as well as diabetes and heart attacks).

TABLE 21

Deaths and death rates, 1921–38

	Total deaths in thousands	Death rate per thousand population	White death rate	Non-white death rate
1921–5 (ann. av.)	1144	11.7	11.2	16.3
1926–8 (ann. av.)	1300	11.8	11.3	17.1
1929	1386	11.9	11.3	16.9
1930	1343	11.3	10.8	16.3
1931	1322	11.1	10.6	15.5
1932	1308	10.9	10.5	14.5
1933	1342	10.7	10.3	14.1
1934–8 (ann. av.)	1420	11.1	10.7	14.7

IV GOVERNMENT AND THE DEPRESSION 1931–2

Many commentators have found the attacks made upon the Hoover Government during the election campaign of 1932 by the Democratic Party candidate, F. D. Roosevelt, ironical. Hoover was assailed with charges of profligacy and of leading the country,

* In 1930 8.6 per cent of the population was aged sixty years or over (and therefore more likely to be adding to the death figures) compared with 7.6 per cent in 1920 and 6.9 per cent in 1910.

through his over-spending, on the road to ruin; he was a meddler, refusing to allow economic nature to take its course : 'It is an administration that has piled bureau on bureau, commission on commission. . . .'

Deficits resulted both in 1931 and 1932 from the federal government's failure to balance expenditure and revenue, reaching over $2½ million in 1932, a deficit substantially exceeded only twice, in 1934 and 1936, during the New Deal years (see Table 25, p. 143). This was mainly the consequence of the drastic fall in government income which followed as an inevitable consequence of the depression of incomes and profits. But is is also to the credit of the Hoover administration that it did not cut back federal expenditure in the face of this decline. Indeed, the stability of expenditure in the 1920s (see Table 19, p. 82) was replaced by an accelerating growth.

In a different context, the economic record of the Hoover government would appear quite remarkable. It authorised the spending of nearly three times more on public buildings in four years ($700 million) than was spent in the thirty years after 1900 ($250 million); 37,000 miles of federally aided roads were built; the area of national parks was increased by 40 per cent and two and a half million acres were added to national forests; the earlier work of President Theodore Roosevelt in the field of conservation (which greatly appealed to Hoover, the engineer) was followed up with the appointment of commissions to examine the uses of oil, water, coal, grazing land and other resources; the Boulder Dam in Arizona (later called the Hoover Dam) was begun in 1930, to be completed under the New Deal, and the plans for the Grand Coolee Dam in Washington State were ready by the end of the administration.

In June 1929, before the Wall Street crash, the *Agricultural Marketing Act* set up an advisory body, the Federal Farm Board, partly in response to pressures from farm co-operatives. The purpose of the F.F.B. was essentially to promote co-operative marketing; its method was to use its $500 million appropriation to make loans to co-operative Stabilization Corporations which would buy up surplus crops in order to maintain their prices; three major commodities, cotton, wool and wheat, were included in the programme through Stabilization Corporations set up in 1930. As with the earlier McNary–Haugen proposals, the main weaknesses of the scheme was that it appeared to promise farmers that their output would be bought up however much they produced, regardless of demand conditions and, apart from a vague 'educational campaign' to preach crop restriction, the Board did nothing to limit output. Consequently the corporations accumulated unwanted stocks which in 1931 were unloaded on the market and forced prices down even further. Nevertheless the lesson was a useful one and the principles behind the Stabilization Corporations did in fact foreshadow the later 'ever-normal granary' concept of the second Agricultural Adjustment Act of 1938.

In the middle of 1930 Hoover agreed to the notorious *Hawley–Smoot Tariff Act* which raised American tariffs to their highest ever. Hoover took no part in encouraging the bill and was probably opposed to it; he was however unwilling to veto it. What was said earlier (p. 81) about the real effects of American tariffs on imports applies equally well to Hawley–Smoot. But it was internationally regarded as a declaration of economic war, the first step in the retreat into autarky by almost all countries in the world. By 1932 two dozen foreign governments had retaliated with tariffs of their own, with quotas and specifically anti-American embargoes and, for these and other reasons, American exports fell by half. A further indirect consequence was that, in reaction to the foreign embargoes on their products, American companies jumped the barriers by setting up subsidiaries in the foreign countries themselves; in the first two years after Hawley–Smoot, some 250 factories were opened in foreign countries by American industrialists. Thus a powerful boost had unwittingly been given to the growth of multi-national corporations. To say, however, that the main damage was done by those who over-reacted to the Hawley–Smoot Tariff does not exonerate its originators from blame.

The main type of aid proposed during the Hoover period was aimed at the restoration of confidence via the financial institutions. Early in October 1931 Hoover persuaded commercial bankers to form the *National Credit Corporation*, using $500 million of their own money, for the purpose of helping banks in distress. Although the Corporation was set up, its funds were quite insufficient and its activities were ineffective. A similiar body, the *Railroad Credit Corporation*, with similar ends and means produced similar non-results.

Only when the Federal Government itself began to offer finance was any, albeit limited, success achieved. The best-known agency was the *Reconstruction Finance Corporation* (R.F.C.) which began its operations in February 1932.

The federal government provided a capital of $500 million and loans at first authorised at $1.5 billion (but later increased to $3.3 billion). These funds were to be used for loans to banks and bank liquidators, insurance companies, savings and loan associations, specified agricultural credit institutions and (when the I.C.C. approved) railroads. In principle the R.F.C. was sound; to provide resources to tide banks, etc., over periods of difficulty and avoid their collapse (with all the dire consequences this would bring). In the period February 1932 to March 1933 the R.F.C. provided loans amounting to $1.4 billion and undoubtedly reduced the volume of liquidations of banks and other finance houses. But the scale and timing of its operations were wrong and the R.F.C. provides the best illustration of the verdict so often passed on Hoover's actions : 'Too little, too late.'

Two other measures need to be noted : the establishment in July 1932 of a system of twelve regional *Federal Home Loan Banks*, to lend to private loan associations. A fund of $125 million provided by the federal government was established, with a somewhat larger contribution from the private institutions who joined as members of the Home Loan Bank System. In the early months of 1933 this body made loans to the relatively trivial total of $22 million. The *Glass–Steagall Banking Act* of February 1932 took an important first step towards enlarging the operations of the Federal Reserve System. It authorised the use of government securities as collateral and effectively liberalised the credit-granting facilities of Federal Reserve Banks. The Act has to be regarded as a precursor to the Glass–Steagall Banking Reform Act of June 1933, during the Hundred Days of the New Deal (see pp. 117–18).

If one is looking for legislative measures in 1932 which foreshadowed the New Deal, then the best illustration is found in a different area of activity, that of labour law. The passage in March 1932 of the *Norris–La Guardia Anti-Injunction Act* was a major landmark in the legal history of American trade unions. Its objects (and effects) were simple : it made illegal the 'yellow-dog' contracts by which workers were engaged for jobs on condition that they did not join a union; and it forbade federal courts from issuing injunctions against organised labour. The seed was thus sown which bore magnificent fruit in the late 1930s.

If the above account suggests that the federal government under Hoover was not so non-interventionist as has often been supposed, the conclusion should not be drawn that Hoover was a crusader for action. By contrast with his immediate predecessors he was willing to use government to a far greater extent than ever before. But by contrast with his successor, Franklin D. Roosevelt, he showed reluctant caution rather than enthusiastic zeal.

V   THE AMERICAN DEPRESSION COMPARED WITH THE BRITISH

Between 1929 and 1932 unemployment in Britain *doubled*, from about 10 per cent to over 20 per cent of the working force. If this increase was catastrophic enough, it was not to be compared with America's experience, a rise from 3 or 4 per cent to around 25 per cent. The differences lay, in other words, not so much in the severity of unemployment at the worst of the depression but in the starting-point.

In sharp contrast with America in the 1920s Britain had never fully recovered from the First World War and had fatalistically come to accept an intractable level of 10 per cent unemployment. While America was revelling in the boom of the 1920s Britain had become accustomed to stagnant sections in her industry, families with no breadwinner and a labour situation which culminated in the General Strike. Full employment, inevitable progress and prosperity were not assumed to be the norm of life in Britain. The years 1929–33 merely aggravated an already serious condition; a slide there was, but not an avalanche; banks did not fail by their thousands; the economic machine never seemed in danger of coming to a complete halt; the unemployed and sick had for nearly a quarter of a century had some insurance benefits to assist them, meagre though they were.

The shock of 1929–33 to American society was far more traumatic. The economic system had, it seemed, utterly collapsed like a row of houses laid flat by a hurricane. What had been thought to be the soundest of foundations had proved incapable of withstanding the onslaught. All former assumptions, all confidence, even all hope of rebuilding, had been swept away.

The psychological damage was at least as serious as the physical. At first it seemed that all that could be done was to see what could be salvaged from the wreckage and to prevent the scavengers and vultures from taking over completely. In this respect, to return to the theme at the very start of this survey, the twenties and the thirties were different worlds.

Another comparison with Britain is also important. British life was sharply divided in the twenties and thirties by the concentration of unemployment into clearly defined geographical and economic regions – the depressed areas. Elsewhere, unemployment was low and life even prosperous, helped by favourable terms of trade which resulted in cheap food. In Britain the depression was divisive, confirming the gulf in the nation between 'haves' and 'have-nots', 'us' and 'them', separating the north and west from the south and east, the 'Celtic fringe' from the 'English' and exacerbating the class divisions in British society already incorporated in the structure of the two major political parties.

The American depression was a shared experience, all-pervasive, sparing no region and no class from its ill-effects and thus politically, economically and socially far less divisive, uniting the nation in a common effort to solve a common problem. Of course there were the fortunates – places and people – who suffered less than their neighbours but, partly because Americans were still (and increasingly) mobile, there were few families wholly unaffected. One of the unifying features was the feeling that now the federal government, and only the federal government, could save the day. Especially in the famous Hundred Days of F. D. Roosevelt, all eyes turned to Washington D.C. and, as a contemporary[4] wrote, 'for the first time the capital feels like the center of the country'. The nation gave to the new President an unprecedented mandate for action. 'Something far more positive than acquiescence vests the President with the authority of a dictator. The authority is a free gift, a sort of unanimous power of attorney. There is a country-wide dumping of responsibility on the federal government.' With this 'country-wide dumping of responsibility' Franklin Roosevelt's appeals for united efforts to combat the depression did not fall on deaf ears.

It would be absurd to pretend that Roosevelt had universal support. Strong personalities generate strong support but also strong enmity. One of the many ironies of the 1930s is to be found in the fanatical hatred and venom, the unreasoning fury far transcending mere political opposition, with which Roosevelt the man (and Mrs Roosevelt) were regarded by many, but above all by the upper stratum of American society, the very group who gained most from Roosevelt's salvage operations.

VI SUGGESTED EXPLANATIONS OF THE GREAT DEPRESSION

Now that the events of 1929–32 and the contrast between the American and British experience have been examined, we may return to a consideration of the causes of the depression. The Wall Street crash came as no surprise to many. As seen earlier, it was welcomed by observers like Keynes in England who, believing the rest of the economy to be fundamentally sound, felt that the collapse would wipe out unhealthy speculation and release funds tied up in speculation for real investment. Even when economic activity in general contracted in 1930, there was every expectation that the precedent of 1921–2 would be followed and that the economy would quickly right itself.

The question which needs to be asked is not so much why the Stock Market collapsed in October 1929, or even why the economy went into decline. As was suggested earlier (p. 89), the difficult problem is why the subsequent depression was so severe and so intractable. How does one account for the fact that the United States, with the most productive economy in the world, suffered more than the other industrialised nations? There is still no general agreement on the answers but a brief summary will now be given of some of the views taken by contemporary and later writers.

1 'Trade cycle' interpretations

Many economists warned in the 1920s that prosperity could not last for ever, that trade cycles were part of the natural order of things, that depression, or at least readjustment, always followed expansion. Some later writers have similarly interpreted the collapse of 1929 as merely another episode in a regular pattern of cyclical behaviour. Historians are disinclined to accept this 'inevitability' explanation since their instinct is to try to identify the unique features in each set of circumstances. But even if one does regard the events of 1929–33 merely as the downswing in a recurring pattern of fluctuations, the questions asked above remain unanswered. More helpful is a cyclical interpretation which accepts the view that there is no such thing as *the* business cycle but asserts that there are several types of cycle, all of differing durations. In this approach the severity and length of the depression are attributable in part, or wholly, to the fact that several of these different but regular cycles all culminated in the peak of the late twenties and all declined together from 1930 on. To express in simplified form the sophisticated arguments involved in this kind of trade-cycle analysis,[5] the kinds of cycles which may be held to fit into this explanation may be summarised as follows : the minor (or 'Kitchin' cycle), average duration 40 months; the major (or 'Juglar' cycle), average duration 9–10 years; the building (or 'Kuznets' cycle), average duration 20 years; the long (or 'Kondratieff' cycle), average duration 50 years.

After 1929 the severity of 'normal' cyclical contractions (the minor and the major cycles) was strongly reinforced, with catastrophic results, by the fact that the two other independent cycles coincidentally peaked at roughly the same time. Building construction, always a substantial proportion of total capital investment, had been a crucial element in the boom of the 1920s but by the mid-1920s had ceased to expand and eventually began to contract (see above, p. 58). The theory of the long-swing assumes that growth is associated with 'block development' resulting from one or more major innovations. In the period up to 1929 there had been two such stimulants, the rise of the automobile industry and electrification, but by 1929 both these expansive forces had reached saturation point and there were no further potential areas of major innovation which could replace them. (For further discussion of the importance of innovation, see below, Section 3, pp. 105–7.) Thus, after 1929 all the cyclical tendencies were strongly downward, one reinforcing another with inexorable pressure.

2 Monetary interpretations

For some economists monetary factors are of paramount importance in explaining economic fluctuations. In its crudest form this theory saw the world-wide depression as the result of a general shortage of gold caused by the decline in world production of gold in the 1920s, eventually bringing the international recovery of the 1920s to a halt.

There is no simple interpretation of the events in America. In the twenties her gold stock increased by half, partly because of Britain's return to the Gold Standard at too high a parity. Whether or not it was the intention of the Federal Reserve Board (see above, pp. 83–5)

American prices remained relatively stable. On the one hand, the influx of gold did not result in an automatic increase in circulating currency (as the 'rules' of the pre-1914 Gold Standard would have required), bringing about a rise in internal prices and so offsetting the over-favourable balance of trade. On the other hand, the falling costs of production did not result in a general reduction of prices. Thus the maintenance of constant prices in the 1920s, when they should have been falling because of higher productivity, amounted to concealed inflation.

From an international viewpoint the fact that the inflation was concealed may be regarded as a de-stabilising influence on the world economy, given America's large balance-of-trade surplus. From a purely internal viewpoint, the maintenance of prices in the 1920s, when reductions should have been occurring, may be regarded as an important element in the eventual failure of internal demand. This weakness was then compounded in the middle months of 1931 by the ill-conceived contraction of the money supply which precipitated the final crisis.

3 The 'stagnation' hypothesis

Writing in the mid-1930s, and reflecting some of the views of his British contemporary, J. M. Keynes, Alvin Hansen saw the American depression as a situation of economic 'stagnation' with investment opportunities temporarily, or even permanently, exhausted. The theoretical background is the Keynesian view that economies stagnate if there are no investment opportunities. Investment generates saving but, no matter how high (or low) the propensity to save, no automatic mechanism maintains the level of investment at the level of saving.

In Hansen's interpretation the key to the depression lay in a historic conjuncture of several circumstances all of which contributed to produce a stagnation of investment. America was no longer an economy in the process of development; she had reached 'maturity', and stagnation was the result. The circumstances to which Hansen (and similar writers) drew attention were the following :

(i) The rate of population growth was now seriously declining with a resultant depressive effect on demand.

(ii) 1929 marked the final 'closing' of the frontier, so that the stimulus to growth created by expansive development had disappeared.

(iii) With the end of the boom associated with the rise of the automobile industry and with electrification, no new and revolutionary innovations were in the offing to take over their dynamic role. There was in other words a dearth of new industries (and thus a lack of investment opportunities) to replace the old ones (see above, p. 103).

(iv) Capital equipment was becoming more efficient so that less was needed to produce a given output, i.e. the capital-output ratio was falling.

(v) The great corporations now had sufficient funds to capitalise themselves without recourse to the capital market.

(vi) In these conditions savings continued to accumulate, but were required only for repairs and replacement.

These items appear to add up to a formidable catalogue of depressive circumstances but, while they certainly help to identify important strategic factors, they depend on a number of assumptions:

(i) The connections between population growth and changes in the rate of economic growth are very complex. A direct causal relationship between a deceleration of population growth and a deceleration (or stagnation) in effective demand cannot be assumed in all circumstances. There is no *a priori* reason why effective demand should not grow just as rapidly via an increase in the propensity to consume of a given population (e.g. by income redistribution; see above, pp. 65–8) as via the impetus derived from the marginal propensity to consume of the additional members of a rapidly growing population.

(ii) The 'frontier' is a concept capable of meaning all things to all men; likewise the 'closing of the frontier'. If the frontier is thought of primarily in terms of human mobility, then it is relevant to note that since 1940 the American people have been more mobile than ever before; more people are shown to be living outside their state of birth in the Censuses of 1950, 1960 and 1970 than in any previous Census, including all those of the nineteenth century when the movement into new 'frontier' lands was at its height. If frontier expansion is understood mainly as creating a need for investment in transport building, then the argument is similarly invalid because, without a frontier, such investment has proceeded apace since 1940 both with the continued extension and improvement of road transport, and even more with air transport. If the 'frontier' means the availability of new agricultural land, then it *is* arguable that this supply came to an effective end in 1929. As the earlier discussion of agricultural problems (pp. 27–30, 59–61) should have indicated, however, the reasons for the calamitous conditions of American agriculture in the thirties were much too complex and varied to be accounted for simply on the grounds that new land was no longer available, though in certain regions of soil exhaustion this must have appeared at the time as a serious problem. If the belief in the existence of a 'frontier' is thought of as creating a certain state of mind, the proposition at once moves into the realm of social psychology and becomes extremely difficult to measure, but may provide a more suggestive approach. In so far as views which may vaguely be termed a 'frontier mentality' involved attitudes towards risk-taking, profit-making and labour they may be considered to have influenced behaviour in the 1920s in ways inappropriate to the economic needs of the time. But whether such American attitudes in the nineteenth century can be regarded as the outcome of frontier expansion is a moot point which has been much debated in historical literature.

(iii) The argument that there was a lack of innovations may be more convincing, though we are confronted with the difficulty of proving a negative. Economists differentiate between invention and innovation, the potential and the actual. The actuality certainly was that there was no powerful emergence of new industries from the late 1920s on, but we cannot deduce from this that there was no potential for innovation, in the form of new techniques and products, which might have been transformed into actuality if economic conditions had been more propitious. Several of the main growth areas after 1945 were based on inventions which were known at least in embryonic form in the 1930s but whose translation into action awaited the return of a healthier economic environment.

The evidence is inconclusive, but this item at any rate merits serious consideration.

(iv), (v), (vi) The final three points are rather more technical and all have an element of truth in them (though some economists might be reluctant to admit even to this; there are those who assume that the capital-output ratio is a constant, despite historical evidence to the contrary).

The 'stagnation' thesis was one that in the 1930s commended itself very widely. Some interpreted the stagnation they observed as permanent ('secular stagnation') and as the ultimate fate awaiting all capitalist economies. Others saw in the situation elements of a temporary stagnation which would eventually be overcome (but as the 1930s wore on, 'eventually' seemed to recede into the remote future). As a mere descriptive statement, however, it is difficult to deny the appropriateness of the expression 'temporary stagnation' to American conditions in the 1930s. Roosevelt had in fact come very close to it himself in a campaign speech of 1932 :

> Equality of opportunity as we have known it no longer exists. Our industrial plant is built; the problem just now is whether under existing conditions it is not overbuilt. Our last frontier has long since been reached, and there is practically no more free land. . . . There is no safety valve in the form of Western prairie to which those thrown out of work by the Eastern economic machines can go for a new start. We are not able to invite the immigration from Europe to share our endless plenty. We are now providing a drab living for our own people.[6]

4   Sectoral imbalance

Other writers have attached particular significance to the weakness of the primary-producing sectors of the American economy. As seen earlier (Chapter 2, Section II) the terms of the trade were unfavourable to primary producers throughout the world during the whole inter-war period. In the United States the events of 1929–33 greatly exacerbated the agricultural problems already present in the 1920s. The fall in the prices of primary products was extremely violent, varying between 30 per cent and 60 per cent according to the item, and farm incomes fell catastrophically. Added to this was the associated collapse of rural banks; most of the 5000 banking failures between 1929 and 1933 were in rural areas, or small towns. These bankruptcies reduced the local supply of money and thus reinforced still further the national contraction of the currency. This decline in farm incomes and rural liquidity greatly reduced the purchasing power of the rural community and thus the demand for the products of the industrial sector.

The ramifications of these combined circumstances were widespread. The bank failures were trebly deflationary by destroying money, encouraging hoarding and discouraging investment. While they can hardly be regarded as decisive in determining both the severity and the long duration of the depression, these circumstances must be included in that powerful conjuncture of forces which combined to depress the economy, especially in those critical months after mid-1931.

So much for the economic imbalance. Far less attention has been paid in the relevant literature to the associated demographic imbalance which was discussed earlier (Chapter 2, Section IV and Chapter 3, Sections III). Let us suffice here merely to recapitulate the points made :

(i) Rural families (the producers) were typically larger than urban families (the consumers), and this feature became more noticeable as urban family size fell still further in the inter-war years.

(ii) Improvements in agricultural productivity made desirable a reduction in the number of farms, but acreage for some crops actually increased in the 1920s.

(iii) Farm families showed a marked reluctance to leave agriculture even in the 1920s. Positive inducements to leave agriculture were slight. The mythology of the moral superiority of rural life over urban life still persisted. But above all towns, and especially small towns, were not growing at a rate rapid enough to absorb, and provide employment opportunities for, the excess members of the agricultural community.

(iv) The two themes cannot be dissociated : low farm income, inadequate opportunities for employment outside agriculture and slow growth of urban demand for farm products were all reinforced by the continuing and probably worsening demographic imbalance.

In the final analysis, however, the weakness of the primary sector merely reflects the lack of strength in the rest of the economy. It is in the secondary and tertiary sectors of economic life that the dynamism must be sought, primary producers usually being obliged to react somewhat passively to circumstances outside their control. Different estimates have been made of the relative growth rates needed in the non-agricultural sectors to maintain favourable terms of trade for primary producers; one of these, for example, has suggested that the non-agricultural sector of the American economy needs to expand at three times the rate of the agricultural sector.

Even if one does not accept such numerical precision, the proposition may still be advanced that even though the industrial and service sectors both expanded massively during the 1920s their growth rate was insufficient to meet the needs of the primary sector. Not enough demand for primary produce was being generated to sustain the income of primary producers. Not enough jobs were being created outside agriculture to take in the surplus labour being created within agriculture both by high farm productivity and high human fertility. The failure of the small towns to grow in the 1920s may thus offer an important clue to the riddle.

5 Conclusion

Perhaps the most satisfactory answer lies in a combination of the last two hypotheses, since the 'stagnation' of the secondary and tertiary sectors is an important part of the total 'imbalance'. The argument may be reduced to the following propositions :

(i) The weakness of the agricultural sector was a symptom of the inadequacy of the rate of expansion of the rest of the economy. The apparently great dynamism of the urban industrial sectors in the 1920s conceals the fact that their expansion fell short of what circumstances required, with the given, and changing, industrial technology and with the given inflated size of the farm sector and its great resistance to contraction.

(ii) This deficiency in the expansion of the twenties was eventually transformed into a curtailment of investment, signs of which were already visible before the Wall Street crash of 1929. By the end of 1931 the incipient contraction had been transformed into a general reluctance to invest at all. That transformation was in the last analysis a failure of confidence.

(iii) This failure of confidence was partly the result of the slowness of the readjustment of outlooks away from the old assumptions that quick profits were the natural reward for enterprise. Falling profitability reinforced the growing belief that the century-old opportunities for expansion were at last over. The slowing down of market expansion, reflecting in particular the slowing down of urban growth, together with the absence of major innovatory developments created an impression that the limitless opportunities of the past had gone for ever. What disappeared was faith in the future, the belief that in the very nature of things next year would be better than this. Thus restoration of confidence was the prime necessity of the early 1930s.

(iv) The nineteenth-century preconditions of, and assumptions about, economic expansion needed to be replaced by a restored belief that under new and different conditions there could be steady development without stagnation. Instant profits could no longer be expected but had to be sought in the long run, to be measured in years and decades rather than months or weeks – a necessity emphasised by the need, growing ever since the 1890s, for long-term planning and investment in the huge capital outlays required by the new technology of the twentieth century. By definition such long-term planning required confidence in the future.

(v) For economic health, the acceleration of the growth of the non-agricultural sectors of the economy needed to be accompanied by the socially painful and politically difficult contraction of the agricultural sector. Such a process could similarly only occur if accompanied by fundamental changes of outlook.

(vi) Finally, the difficulties of readjustment were greatly hampered in the early 1930s by the shortcomings of American economic institutions. Part of any process of economic rehabilitation necessitated the removal of the many institutional frictions that impeded the transformations required.

5

The New Deal: Origins and Measures

I FRANKLIN DELANO ROOSEVELT

The economic depression of 1929–33 was at its worst during the election campaign of 1932. When Franklin D. Roosevelt was nominated as the candidate of the Democratic Party for the presidency on 1 July 1932, there were some 12 million or more persons unemployed out of a total work force of 50 million – about one in every four. Countless others were under-employed, and estimates of the numbers receiving public or private charity vary between 25 and 30 million. In January of that year Roosevelt had commented : 'Make no mistake about it. I do not know why anyone should want to be President, with things in the shape they are now.'

Franklin Delano Roosevelt, a distant cousin of former President Theodore Roosevelt, had been in public life for over twenty years. He had entered the Senate of the State of New York in 1910 at the age of twenty-eight. Familiar as we are with photographs of a dying Roosevelt taken at the Yalta Conference in 1945, it is easy to forget that when he took office Roosevelt was one of the younger American Presidents. Although he was the only American to serve as President for more than two terms – entering his fourth term in 1945 – he was still only sixty-three years old when he died, not much above the age at which several Presidents (including Truman and Eisenhower) first took office.

From 1913 to 1920, Roosevelt was Assistant Secretary of the Navy in Woodrow Wilson's cabinet and ran as Democratic nominee for the vice-presidency in 1920. In August 1921 (aged thirty-nine) he was stricken with poliomyelitis and heavily paralysed. After a near-miraculous recovery he returned to public life to be elected Governor of New York State in 1928.

At first Roosevelt's nomination was not particularly popular, but gradually he began to impose his dynamic personality on the election. That personality must be the starting-point for any discussion of the New Deal. It was his chief asset and became a symbol of hope to Americans (and later in the Second World War to Western Europeans). In the words of Raymond Moley, one of his advisers : 'I liked Franklin Roosevelt for the same reason that millions of other people were soon to like him – for his vibrant aliveness, his warmth, his sympathy, his activism; I had faith in him. The rest did not precede this; it followed.'

The personality of F.D.R. soon came to dominate the American political scene, even to the extent of transcending the massive economic problems of the day. Magnified and amplified by press, radio and cinema in a manner enjoyed (or suffered) by no previous President, Roosevelt's voice, grin and radiant confidence became factors in the situation as real as the bank failures and bread lines. During the 1930s an unprecedented extension of the mass media of communication personalised American politics as never before and in particular concentrated on the embodiment of the nation in the figure of the President. F.D.R. made particularly good use of the radio in his 'fireside chats', his seemingly private talks with every person in the nation who cared to listen.

As the election proceeded, Roosevelt stated his belief in the need for action. Exactly what action was not made clear, but some action there would be. One campaign speech included the famous declaration : 'The country needs and, unless I mistake its temper, the country demands, bold, persistent experimentation. It is common sense to take a method and try it. If it fails admit it frankly and try another. But above all try something.' This extract well summarises Roosevelt's eventual approach as President to the problems of the depression : 'bold, persistent experimentation'* and a willingness to abandon one method and try another. The key to this approach may lie in Roosevelt's own personal history, with his conquest of his own crippling polio. He often used medical metaphors when speaking of his policies to which he gave the name Dr New Deal. He had fought his way back to life from his paralysis through sheer willpower and through trying a whole series of different remedies recommended by his doctors. The same methods would bring

* This was not Roosevelt's first use of the phrase. Before his nomination, speaking as Governor of New York State, he had used the identical words, 'bold, persistent experimentation' with different measures for bringing about economic recovery, in a radio speech in April 1932.

America back to life again. Sheer will-power (in his Inaugural Address he asked, 'Will the American people overcome the Depression?' and answered his own question quite simply : 'They will, if they want to') would be combined with experiments with different remedies until the right one, or the right combination, was discovered which would prove to have the requisite healing qualities ('bold, persistent experimentation : if it fails . . . try another. . . . But above all try simething').

The policy was thus to be pragmatic, proceeding by trial through error to fresh trial. It is a mistake to think of the New Deal as a policy or a coherent group of consistent policies. At no time did a New Deal programme of action exist as a uniform campaign strategy. Rather it was a collection of expedients, some designed on the spot to meet a given situation, others drawing on earlier theories or practices. This aspect of the New Deal is well summarised in the words of a great Roosevelt admirer, A. M. Schlesinger Jr, 'F.D.R.'s basic pragmatism verged at times on improvization for the sake of improvization, an addiction to playing my ear in the nervous conviction that any kind of noise is better than silence.'

II ELECTION, INTERREGNUM AND INAUGURATION

As the election campaign of 1932 proceeded, Roosevelt gathered around him a group of advisers, mostly university professors, who came to constitute his famous 'Brains Trust' : Raymond Moley, A. A. Berle, Rexford Tugwell, Samuel Rosenman; in addition he called in for consultation Harry Hopkins, Bernard Baruch, William Green, Colonel House and others. Their viewpoints and the counsel they gave differed. But two general attitudes seemed to emerge : first, that the federal government should unequivocally assume responsibility for the economic condition of the nation, and act; second, that the normal principle of private housekeeping – that you do not spend more than your income allows – should be applied at the national level, i.e. that there should be no departure from the traditional policy of balancing the budget.

Roosevelt's 1932 victory was as great as Harding's in 1920 : he won 22.8 million votes and 42 states to Hoover's 15.7 million votes and 6 states. As Table 22 indicates, Democratic dominance in the 1930s was even stronger than Republic dominance had been in the 1920s (cf. above, Table 10), especially after 1936.

TABLE 22

The election results, 1932–8

A. The Presidency

Year	President	Vice-President	Party	Per cent share of votes cast
1932	Roosevelt	Garner	Dem.	57.4
1936	Roosevelt	Garner	Dem.	60.8

B. The Congress

	Senate			House of Representatives		
	Dem.	Rep.	Other	Dem.	Rep.	Other
1932	60	35	1	310	117	5
1934	69	25	2	319	103	10
1936	76	16	4	331	87	13
1938	69	23	4	261	164	4

A defeated American President does not pack his bags immediately and creep out by the side-door of the White House as surreptitiously as possible, but remains in office until his successor is sworn in at an official Inauguration ceremony. Until the period of waiting was shortened to two months,* the victorious candidate had to endure a four-month purgatory between the election in November and his assumption of office the following March.

This delay of the Interregnum was particularly damaging to the American economy in the winter of 1932–3. Neither the defeated Hoover nor the victorious Roosevelt could exert authority and conditions continued to deteriorate. For four uneasy months the ship appeared to be drifting helplessly without a captain. There was virtually no co-operation between Roosevelt and the retiring administration. Farm prices continued to fall, unemployment continued to rise. The banking situation steadily worsened. On 30 January – Roosevelt's fifty-first birthday – Adolf Hitler was appointed Chancellor of Germany and on 15 February, in Miami, Joseph Zangara failed in his attempt to assassinate the President-elect (but his shots hit others, and killed the Mayor of Chicago).

At last on 4 March 1933 came the day of Franklin D. Roosevelt's Inauguration as President. His Inaugural Address was a rallying

* By the Twentieth Amendment to the Constitution which came into effect in February 1933, too late to affect Roosevelt's first Inauguration.

call as inspiring and to become as famous as any of Winston Churchill's wartime speeches : 'Let me assert my firm belief that the only thing we have to fear is fear itself. . . . We must act and act quickly. . . . We do not distrust the future of social democracy. The people of the United States have not failed.' None of these propositions was self-evident in March 1933 and it needed a leader of Roosevelt's calibre to proclaim them.

III ROOSEVELT'S ASSUMPTIONS AND AIMS

As already observed, Roosevelt did not assume office with a clear set of proposals awaiting execution. In his campaign he had expressed negative disapproval of Hoover's do-nothingism more coherently than he had formulated precise prescriptions for his own do-somethingism.

But one difference in approach was clear. Hoover excused his own reluctance to act on the grounds that the depression was attributable to international factors and could only be cured by international measures. Roosevelt by contrast argued that the cause of the depresion lay within the American economy and therefore could and should be cured by domestic measures. This was a false dichotomy. As observed earlier, such phenomena as the low returns to primary producers were international; so also was the instability of the money markets, dating far back into the previous decade.

Roosevelt's approach to the depression was essentially introspective, concentrating on the internal economy and turning his back on the outside world. Among his first actions was America's withdrawal from the World Economic Conference in London. In the summer of 1932 the major European powers had sponsored this conference through the League of Nations and Hoover had agreed to American participation. In April 1933, soon after his Inauguration, Roosevelt brought America off the Gold Standard. In June the American delegation led by Cordell Hull arrived in London for the negotiations, but early in July Roosevelt sent a message which amounted to American repudiation of the conference. This did not survive the American withdrawal, despite attempts to salvage the wreckage. Thus the hopes, meagre as they were in 1933, of even a first start in the direction of world economic co-operation were condemned to frustration. The United States withdrew behind the Maginot Line of her tariff barriers. Autarky became the watchword of the 1930s, whether of the variety of Dr Schacht in Germany or the National government in Britain, but with the United States leading the way, first with the Hawley–Smoot Tariff of 1930 and then with Roosevelt's retreat still further into economic isolationism.

In this respect at least, the philosophy of the New Deal was clear. The American nation was to achieve security and welfare by re-ordering the domestic economy without any real concern for events outside America. This being so, the internal aims could be defined as the three Rs : relief, recovery and reform.

The first, immediate and urgent requirement was *relief* : to alleviate, by any and all means available, the hardships and often desperate suffering caused by the depression. This included the need to prevent any further deterioration of the economic situation. Secondly, in the middle distance, the task was in induce a *recovery* of the economic system; if the decline could be halted, this was only the beginning. A fresh process of expansion had to be started and unemployment drastically reduced. Thirdly, and for the long term, the need was to *reform* the institutional and other weaknesses in the American economy; initially to prevent the recurrence of a breakdown similar to that of 1929, and subsequently to create mechanisms that would enable future governments to pursue constructive and effective economic policies.

IV THE HUNDRED DAYS

The four months which followed Roosevelt's arrival in the White House saw intense, feverish activity on the part of the Government. Let us briefly examine the main actions taken during that Hundred Days period.

1 Banking

Five days after Roosevelt's Inauguration, on 9 March 1933, all banks were forced to close through the proclamation of a four-day bank holiday. In three years to December 1932 over 4000 banks had failed. As observed in the last chapter, most of these were in rural communities where the collapse of the local bank brought great loss to the local inhabitants by destroying all their assets.. These failures had eroded confidence : people hoarded their money rather than entrust it to the banks.

In 1932 the Reconstruction Finance Corporation had been set up under Hoover to lend funds to banks in difficulty, but the failures still continued. Early in 1933 several state governments had taken matters into their own hands by declaring bank holidays in their own states.

Roosevelt's first week in office was in fact dominated by the banking crisis; his first fireside chat over the radio on 12 March began, 'I want to talk for a few minutes with the people of the United States about banking . . .'

Once the banks were closed, they were only allowed to re-open if and when they could demonstrate their credit-worthiness to Treasury officials who worked round the clock in their examinations. Within a week banks were re-opening but with public confidence established that those which were now in operation could be trusted. Already by 16 March three-quarters of all banks within the Federal Reserve System had re-opened and within a month about three-quarters of non-member banks had followed suit.

These initial emergency measures were shortly followed up by more permanent changes in the banking system. On 21 June 1933 Roosevelt signed the *Glass–Steagall Banking Reform Act* whose provisions were as follows :

(i) The power of the Federal Reserve Board was increased to enable it to refuse credit to banks making excessive speculative loans.

(ii) Member banks within the Federal Reserve System were forbidden to pay interest on demand deposits, to discourage them from making speculative loans.

(iii) Investment banking was to be separated from commercial banking in order to destroy the affiliate system and force every bank to decide which type of business it would engage in (and J. P. Morgan and Company subsequently elected to drop its investment business and become a commercial bank).

(iv) Most important of all, the *Federal Deposit Insurance Corporation* (F.D.I.C.) was set up to guarantee bank deposits. The bankruptcies of the previous years had wiped out the life savings of thousands of ordinary people. The F.D.I.C. now offered an insurance on all deposits up to $2500 (in 1935 this was raised to $5000 and by October 1966 the insured figure had reached $15,000).

Bank failures in the decade after 1933 declined sharply. A total of 450 failures occurred in the seven years 1934–40, a lower figure than that of any *single* year between 1923 and 1933 (e.g. 1927 had over 650 bank failures); 350 of those failures were of F.D.I.C.-insured banks, so that the effects of these bankruptcies were minimised.

2 Economy measures

Like so many banks in 1933, the federal government itself appeared to be heading for bankruptcy. By this time it received about two-thirds of all its revenue from individual and corporation income-tax. As the depression lowered private incomes, government revenue automatically declined. In 1929 individual and corporation income-taxes each yielded over $1 billion; by 1933 both were yielding below $0.4 billion. The Government's total revenue from all sources in 1932 and 1933 was almost exactly half what it had been in 1927, 1928, 1929 and 1930.

Roosevelt had promised in his election campaign to balance the nation's budget in accordance with the orthodox financial principles of the time. With government revenue down by half, it appeared that the only practicable policy was to cut expenditure.

Accordingly on 11 March, one week after the Inauguration, the House of Representatives agreed to the *Economy Bill* prepared by Roosevelt's budget director, Lewis W. Douglas. The disablement pensions of war veterans were halved, congressional salaries and the salaries of all federal employees reduced together with other federal expenditures; the target was to save a total of $½ billion.

The Economy Bill of March 1933 provides the first of many examples of the inconsistencies of the New Deal. It operated both against the policy of providing relief (since pension reductions brought social hardship to recipients), and also militated against the objective of recovery by curtailing government expenditure and reducing individual purchasing power. In the light of Keynesian economics, these measures of retrenchment can only be regarded as unfortunate, aggravating rather than alleviating the nation's economic plight.

3 Agriculture

The problems facing the American farmer as far back as the 1920s were examined in earlier chapters. The fall in farm incomes was one of the most serious aspects of the depression years.

A hastily contrived bill, mainly the work of Roosevelt's Secretary of Agriculture, Henry A. Wallace, was presented to Congress in March and eventually signed into law by the President on 12 May 1933. This was the first *Agricultural Adjustment Act*, or the Triple A. The intention behind this measure was to restore farm incomes by raising farm prices; this was to be done by removing the glut of produce on the markets through the deliberate restriction of farm production. Farmers would accordingly be paid to reduce their output of 'basic' crops. Under the terms of this Act :

(i) The Agricultural Adjustment Administration (A.A.A.) was set up with the task of raising farm prices through the restriction of output.

(ii) The A.A.A. would decide on an 'acreage allotment', the amount of each 'basic' crop to be planted in the next season. The total acreage for each group was subdivided into acreage allocations for individual farms, proportionate to the quantity they had produced in the recent past. 'Benefit payments' were then assessed and paid to farmers in accordance with the reduced size of their production. The scheme applied to wheat, cotton, field corn, hogs, rice, tobacco and dairy produce (and in 1934 the list was extended).

(iii) The cost of these payments was to be met, not out of the general exchequer, but out of a new processing tax to be paid by food manufacturers. (For example, millers were to pay a tax on every bushel of wheat they turned into flour.)

Through the summer of 1933 the acreage-reduction policy was translated by farmers into action : 10 million acres of cotton were ploughed in; 6 million hogs were slaughtered and so forth. The results were not entirely as expected. The public was angered at the sight of crop destruction, especially of foodstuffs, when people were starving. True, many farmers producing 'basic' crops received 'benefit payments', but others were not covered by the list. Moreover, what farmers did with this new income was not always to the advantage of the national economy : some of the bigger farmers used the funds to purchase new machinery, thus improving their own productivity and enabling them to dispense with some of their labour. The policy of raising food prices was not conducive to increasing demand for agricultural produce and in this respect did nothing to help the problem of under-consumption.

Another important agricultural measure was the establishment of the Farm Credit Administration (F.C.A.) on 19 June 1933 to consolidate all existing rural credit agencies.

Despite Roosevelt's growing impatience, the proposals for industry were not ready for presentation to Congress until 15 May, reaching the President for signature on 16 June. The *National Industrial Recovery Act* (N.I.R.A.) created a new agency, the National Recovery Administration (N.R.A.), with General Hugh S. Johnson as its Administrator, and embodied three main sets of proposals :

(i) Title I of the bill stated its intention 'to promote the organization of industry for the purpose of cooperative action among trade groups'. Codes of 'fair competition' were to be worked out by industrialists in conjunction with the Administration. In effect this meant that industrial producers were encouraged and abetted to move away from competitive price-cutting and instead to make price-fixing agreements. Goods sold at prices thus agreed were indicated to the public by use of the Blue Eagle symbol of the N.R.A. Under this system some 600 basic price codes and 200 supplementary codes were approved. These codes were not promises to avoid price increases (as one might expect in the inflationary environment of the early 1970s) but were undertakings not to *lower* prices, i.e. not to undercut a competitor's selling price and thus create further unemployment. The codes also incorporated maximum hour and minimum wage agreements. The price-fixing codes of the N.R.A. implied a repudiation of the policy originally established by the Sherman Act and subsequently pursued with varying degrees of enthusiasm and success. The anti-trust legislation remained in force but was pushed into the background by the Blue Eagle policy.

(ii) The second part of the bill (Title II) set up a *Public Works Administration* (P.W.A.) with an appropriation of $3.3 billion to promote heavy-construction projects in the general interest and, to Hugh Johnson's disappointment, Harold Ickes was placed at its head. As P.W.A. came into operation, Ickes was only prepared to authorise expenditure after careful and thorough investigation of all proposals. Projects had to be 'self-liquidating'; i.e. they had to offer the promise that they would in the long run pay for themselves. Thus those looking for quick results did not find them in P.W.A., as many months, sometimes years, elapsed before any project got under way.

By the end of 1933 only $113 million had been spent out of P.W.A.'s $3 billion appropriation, and still only $1 billion by the end of 1934 (when it provided work directly for about three-quarters of a million, though indirectly for many more). It made no noticeable impact on the relief rolls, partly because it had least to offer to those who most needed help. Its undertakings came into operation slowly and were often capital-intensive rather than large employers of labour. The administrators of P.W.A. were obsessed with a fear of holding back recovery by forcing up the price of capital and labour.

(iii) An important section of Title I was the famous Section 7a which dealt with labour relations. This section was subsequently re-enacted in 1935 (when the rest of the N.I.R.A. was abandoned after the Supreme Court decision in the Schechter Case, see pp. 169–70) as the National Labor Relations Act (or the Wagner Act).

5 The Tennessee Valley Authority

Another measure which fell within the first Hundred Days was the Tennessee Valley Authority Act of May 1933. This was to prove one of the most widely known and spectacular of all New Deal promotions and its most lasting monument. The Act established a Board of three persons entitled the Tennessee Valley Authority, 'to maintain and operate properties owned by the government at Muscle Shoals, Alabama, to develop industry and agriculture in the Tennessee Valley, to improve navigation on the Tennessee and to control the flood waters of the Tennessee and Mississippi rivers'. The Authority was given wide powers to acquire land, build dams and power houses, establish hydro-electric plants, develop programmes for flood control, reafforestation and for the prevention of soil erosion.

The story of the T.V.A. begins in 1918 with the construction of a dam and two nitrate plants at Muscle Shoals on the Tennessee River in Alabama. The intention was to make explosives during the war and fertilisers afterwards. Subsequent attempts to develop this government installation further were unsuccessful, including one vetoed by President Hoover in March 1931 after being passed by Congress. The leading champion of the plan was Senator George W. Norris of Nebraska, after whom the magnificent Norris Dam was eventually and appropriately named.

The T.V.A. has rightly been regarded as a pioneering attempt at regional planning. On the one hand, it had to secure the co-operation of seven different state governments and countless local authorities and on the other it was a multi-purpose body concerned with the co-ordinated development of a vast range of resources. Its ramifications included the teaching of methods of contour ploughing to the hill farmers of the region. It was later to be chosen as the site, during the Second World War, for atomic energy research at Oak Ridge; when the demand for electricity later came to exceed the capacity of the rivers, it turned to the generation of electricity from coal and was thus obliged to turn its interests into mining.

The symbolism of T.V.A. has often mesmerised observers into a facile acceptance of a view that because it was big it must be good. Nevertheless, careful input–output analysis has cast doubt on the economic justification of T.V.A. (as well as of other similarly spectacular hydro-electric developments), though in the very long run their performance will have to be judged in the context of total energy supplies. Until the federal government brought in the Atomic Energy Commission, there was a disappointing response (with the important exception of aluminium) to the hope that cheap electricity would attract industries to the Valley. But the symbolism cannot be undervalued. Within a few years, one of the most backward regions in America had become the second largest producer of power in the country.

6 Employment creation

On 21 March 1933 Roosevelt proposed to Congress three further areas of activity : the provision of direct relief to provide food and clothing by means of federal grants to the states; job creation through the employment by the federal government of workers on immediate projects which would not interfere with private industry; a longer-term public works programme. The implementation of the last of these proposals did not get fully under way until the formation of the Civil Works Administration (C.W.A.) and the Works Progress Administration (W.P.A.).

The main agency in the first of these proposals was the *Federal Emergency Relief Administration* (F.E.R.A.), set up in May under Harry Hopkins. At first F.E.R.A. was concerned with direct transfers of money to the states for relief, to be administered through established welfare channels with social workers playing a leading role. Gradually Hopkins turned towards work provision as a more satisfactory method of providing relief, and already in the summer of 1933 F.E.R.A. was beginning to sponsor improvised 'make-work' projects.

The second objective found its principal expression in the *Civilian Conservation Corps* (C.C.C.), created in April 1933. Employment, primarily in forestry work, was found for thousands, eventually millions, of youths who were lodged in quasi-military camps. The C.C.C. has been accused of having affinity with the Hitler Youth movement, but nevertheless it became and remained one of the most consistently popular of all New Deal agencies. C.C.C. recruits were often able to acquire new skills or gain other educational opportunities; all of them were exposed to a healthy, open-air life. Many an ageing American businessman or professor of today spent some time in his youth doing manual labour as a C.C.C. 'graduate'.

V SUBSEQUENT MEASURES

By the middle of June 1933 the dynamic leadership of the new President, the activity of an energetic Congress, and the sheer toil of hundreds of enthusiastic advisers and law-makers had in one hundred frenetic days launched programmes involving innovations, restrictions, reforms and interventions in practically every branch of economic life. Banking, agriculture, industry, labour, transport, commerce and the credit system were all affected, and special measures were adopted for special areas and problems.

It would have been humanly impossible to maintain the pace of those hectic days, and those who remember them still speak with excitement of the intoxication and enthusiasm – and the physical exhaustion – of the episode. By the summer of 1933, the main areas of activity had been designated and to some extent the main lines of attack drawn up. The years which followed saw the working out of those original measures, a process which involved the abandonment of some and the amplification and refinement of others, as well as serious political and constitutional struggles directly stemming from the New Deal legislation.

The measures introduced in the following years emphasise the view stated earlier that a New Deal never existed in the sense of a unified, co-ordinated programme. Nor is it much more helpful to divide the policies chronologically into a first and a second New Deal. Throughout, Roosevelt and his advisers sought expedients, reacted (though often vigorously) to events (e.g. the large deficit of the financial year 1936), or merely acquiesced in developments originating largely outside their control (e.g. the advance of trade unionism). The measures abounded in contradictions, the actions of the right hand often being nullified by those of the left one. Any search for consistency will be in vain; all that can be found is a conviction that the Federal Government should be active, together with a vague notion that policy ought to aim at helping the under-dog (though all too often measures with precisely that aim had quite different effects).

Without examining all subsequent developments in detail, we cannot leave the New Deal at the *status quo* of June 1933. Both the N.I.R.A. and the A.A.A. were eventually (in 1935) declared unconstitutional by the Supreme Court. This led directly to the confrontation between that body and the President when Roosevelt introduced his court-packing plan. The attitude of the Supreme Court has been the subject of much debate. A popular view has been that the majority of the nine Justices were reactionary old men determined to kill the 'socialistic' measures of the early New Deal but that, after Roosevelt's threat, the Court simply decided to toe the line. From 1936, when a change of sides by one Justice changed the previous voting pattern of 4–5 into 5–4 (and thus 'the switch in time saved nine' from Roosevelt's threat), the Court ceased its opposition to New Deal measures. Yet it would probably be agreed by most writers that the Administration was in fact relieved to be rid of the N.I.R.A. and the A.A.A., neither of which had proved particularly effective. Another view holds that the crucial vote was actually switched *before* Roosevelt's court-packing plan appeared and that the Supreme Court was entirely justified on legal grounds in its decisions; the legislation of the Hundred Days was hastily and often sloppily drawn up and sometimes *did* offend the Constitution. Whether the Justices changed their views for political reasons, whether Congress began to take more care in drafting its legislation, or whether, as Justices retired and F.D.R. appointed his own nominees, the Court simply changed its personnel, the fact is that after 1936 it accepted as legitimate virtually anything the government proposed in the realm of economics. Its agreement to the re-drafted National Labor Relations Act in 1937 was the first clear sign of its new attitude.

An important area in which policy was modified was that of public works. The P.W.A., as already observed, did not generate employment quickly; its effects were achieved with excruciating slowness. Gradually the emphasis shifted to make the creation of work the first objective. The change was seen in the growing ascendancy of Harry Hopkins over Harold Ickes and may be symbolised in the re-arrangement of the letters from P.W.A. to W.P.A.; with the latter, *work* came first.

The first landmark was the establishment in November 1933 of the *Civil Works Administration* (C.W.A.), an emergency measure to see the nation through the first New Deal winter. By February 1934 jobs had been provided for some 4 million. The culmination occurred in the summer of 1935 with the establishment of the *Works Progress Administration* (W.P.A.) (the name of which, just to confuse matters still further, was changed in 1939 to *Work Projects Administration*), under Harry Hopkins, with $5 million granted for unemployment relief. The W.P.A. is best regarded as the logical extension of F.E.R.A. Work provision was now entirely separated from direct relief, the latter being handed back to the states and to local government.

The Federal Government now concentrated on sponsoring 'useful' labour-intensive projects, and road building and improvement was always a strong candidate. But the list of undertakings was very long and included music, writers', art and theatre projects as well as social and economic research (a complete list is given in L. V. Chandler, *America's Greatest Depression, 1929–1941*, pp. 204–5). The legacy handed down included everything from water mains and sewers to guide books : 100,000 public buildings, 287 new airports, 75,000 bridges, $\frac{1}{2}$ million miles of road, as well as post offices, parks, playgrounds and reservoirs. In February 1936 just over 3 million persons were employed in W.P.A. projects and an even higher figure was reached in November 1938. The W.P.A. continued its activities until the middle of 1943 by which time it was estimated to have provided 13,686,000 man-years of employment.

An important long-term measure was the consolidation of earlier, temporary provisions in the Securities Exchange Act of June 1934 which founded the *Securities and Exchange Commission* (S.E.C.). This was an ambitious move to prevent a repetition of the events which had occurred on the Stock Exchange in 1929. The Act set up a Commission of five persons to regulate the Security Exchanges and provide investors with much greater protection. Its powers of regulation included requirements to be fulfilled before any new issue could be offered to the public, and the supervision of trading practices and of investment advisory services. In its subsequent forty-year career the S.E.C. has extended its regulatory scope over other financial practices, including corporation reorganisations.

Another measure of 1934, the *Trade Agreement Act*, gave authorisation to the President to negotiate trade agreements with foreign countries for three-year periods. Under the Act he was granted power to make tariff changes of up to 50 per cent in either direction. This Act was purely permissive, but was subsequently renewed five times and formed the basis for America's gradual departure in the late 1930s from the high tariff level established by Hawley–Smoot.

In addition to the establishment of W.P.A., the year 1935 saw two other major legislative enactments. After the unfavourable Supreme Court decision against the N.I.R.A., its labour provisions were embodied in the *National Labor Relations Act*. This was the second step (Norris–La Guardia being the first) towards providing American trade unions with the basic ground-law of a legal existence. The Act forbade employers to refuse collective bargaining and made it illegal for them to try to put pressure on collective bargaining; they were prohibited from interfering with trade unions in their establishments and from making non-membership (or membership) of a trade union a condition of employment. To enforce the Act, the National Labor Relations Board was established. In April 1937 the Act was upheld by the Supreme Court in a series of decisions and the way was made clear for rapid union growth.

The final Act of importance in 1935 was the *Social Security Act*, the first comprehensive measure in American history intended to involve the federal government directly in welfare provision. Up to this time unemployment and old-age relief had been left to state or local governments, and in 1934 only Wisconsin had full unemployment insurance.

The Act confirmed state responsibility for welfare but involved the federal government through the adoption of the 'matching grant' principle. That is, the federal government agreed to double whatever sums state governments were willing to contribute towards old-age pension schemes, up to $20 per person per month. The Act followed lines similar to those of the 'Lloyd George' (insurance benefits) in Britain : unemployment insurance was to be financed by a tax paid by employers; old-age pension benefits by joint contributions from employers and employees. Additionally the S.S.A. provided for appropriations, again to be administered through grants to the state, for other welfare benefits such as the care of destitute children, medical and surgical services for crippled children, aid for the blind and vocational training for the handicapped.

To complete this brief narrative survey of the later New Deal, mention must be made of the establishment in 1937 of the *U.S. Housing Authority*, with powers to make loans and give federal aid for slum clearance and building low-rent houses. In 1938 the *Fair Labor Standards Act* fixed minimum wages and maximum hours for all employees engaged in inter-state commerce, and set up a wages and hours division within the Department of Labor to administer the Act.

Finally, the year 1938 also saw a major departure in agricultural policy, embodied in the second A.A.A., the *Agricultural Adjustment Act* of 16 February 1938. This was the measure that first introduced the concept of the 'ever-normal granary'. One of the many tragedies of the 1930s was that the economic plight of farmers in many areas was aggravated by a series of natural disasters : the earthquake of 1933 in southern California; the drought and dust storms at the end of 1933 and throughout 1934 that stripped the top-soil of the dust-bowl counties of Oklahoma, Western Texas, Eastern New Mexico and South Kansas and drove hundreds of families off their holdings;* the Ohio floods of 1937; the New England hurricane of 1938 which caused 700 deaths and destroyed two billion trees. Paradoxically when Nature took a hand in such devastating ways the problem shifted sharply and diametrically from crop reduction to the immediate need to increase production sufficiently to keep the farmer and his family alive.

These vicissitudes emphasised the wide fluctuations between years of good and bad harvests. Unused stocks of farm produce might vary from vast surpluses in one year to national, or at least local, shortages in the next. Price supports made matters worse since, by promising a high price for certain products, they encouraged farmers to switch to these irrespective of current demands and also ignored the differing rates of technological improvements in different areas of production. Henry A. Wallace, Secretary of Agriculture,

* The events made familiar to the world in John Steinbeck's novel *The Grapes of Wrath* and the subsequent film based upon it.

had long been attracted by the notion of using the high stocks of one year to balance the shortfall of another and the second A.A.A. attempted to translate the notion into practical measures. The agency made responsible for carrying this out was the Commodity Credit Corporation, a body set up in 1933 but remaining relatively unimportant until 1938. The method of control was the corporation's authority to make loans to farmers on the security of their crops. It was now made mandatory that these loans were at rates based on the 'parity prices' of the period 1910–14 (considered favourable to farmers). The principle was that if the price of the commodity fell, the corporation assumed possession of the surplus crops and the debt was cancelled; if the price rose the farmer paid off the loan and kept the difference, and no stocks accumulated. In other words, the loan rates became minimum prices. With the operation of this system the corporation began to accumulate large stocks of wheat, corn, cotton and tobacco between 1939 and 1941 when production was high and prices low. In the event, these stocks were then available for subsequent sale in the profitable price situation brought about by the Second World War.

6

The New Deal: Success or Failure?

I INTRODUCTION

Several difficulties confront us in attempting an appraisal of the effectiveness of the New Deal. Even the fact of a code name 'New Deal', with the derived term 'New Dealer', creates a barrier; as with all such terms with a quasi-religious symbolism – from 'Corn Laws' to 'Black Power' – the very words assume an emotive significance which inhibits purely rational investigation and assessment. By the late 1960s, the expression 'Old New Dealer' had become a term of abuse in contemporary politics, implying a senile left-over from the 1930s. A second difficulty is the identification of New Deal policies with the personality of President Roosevelt, a man who excited deep feelings both of support and opposition. It is perhaps difficult to admire the man and yet pronounce his policies unsuccessful – or vice versa.

Above all for the British student there are serious dangers of assuming false parallels between the British and American scenes. This is particularly true of the American political system.

(i) The United States is a federation. The federal government (President, Congress, Supreme Court) is America's central government in Washington D.C., but its powers are not directly comparable with those of the British central government at Westminster. There were in this period 48 separate states, with 48 different state governments. The areas of activity of the federal government were laid down in broad terms in the American Constitution of 1787, but were always subject to the interpretations of the Supreme Court. Thus legislation which gave new powers, or new types of power, to the different branches of government could not automatically be regarded as operative until a case had been brought before the Supreme Court to test whether those powers were constitutional.

(ii) The principle of 'division of power' embodied in the American Constitution means that the relationship between the

Executive (President and Cabinet) and Legislature (Congress, i.e. Senate and House of Representatives) is very different from that between a British Prime Minister and Cabinet and the British Parliament. The President is not a member of Congress; nor are his Cabinet, who are his own personal appointees. He cannot directly control measures presented to Congress. Bills originating in either House may be in accord, or may conflict, with presidential policies. The President may wish to frustrate the wishes of Congress (e.g. if his own party is in a minority, or if he believes certain interest groups to be over-represented), and veto legislation for that reason. Some at least of the apparent contradictions in the total package conveniently named the 'New Deal' resulted from the lack of co-ordination between the measures which emanated from Congress, and resulted from the driving force of individual members, and those which were directly sponsored by the White House.

(iii) In its own way the American Senate is as peculiarly constituted as the House of Lords (but certainly in this period wielded more power). Every state, irrespective of population, has two Senators, with the result that states with small populations (which are typically agricultural) are grossly over-represented. Hence in the Senate the economic interest of agriculture and the geographical interest of South and West is excessively powerful, while industrial interests and the urban North-East are seriously under-represented.

(iv) American political customs are difficult to change. They are based rigidly upon a *written* Constitution and written laws. Americans are suspicious of government like the British, based on consensual authority with practices not wholly governed by formal rules, written regulations and laws, but as much by unwritten conventions, accepted codes of behaviour, personal contacts and compacts – the old-boy network. The American founding fathers were pessimistic in their view of human nature and unwilling to leave government subject only to good faith, to the social pressures to conformity (which only operate anyway in a small, closed society where individuals are well known to each other; when you are dealing with strangers, you want something legally binding). They wanted open agreements, openly arrived at and written down; what was permissible was what was written, and what was written was the law; the result inevitably became a lawyer's paradise. In Britain methods of government have often been altered by changing the practice without changing the law, and there is no Supreme Court to pronounce upon the constitutionality of a proposed change.

Part of Roosevelt's problems arose from his practical difficulties in bringing about fundamental change in the methods of government. He was often fighting constitutional battles at the same time as economic battles, fighting on too many fronts at the same time. His pragmatic approach of 'try something, try anything' may be interpreted as reflecting in part at least a real uncertainty as to what the Supreme Court would allow him to do.

(v) The American party system differs from the British in several respects. It is misleading to equate the American political alignments for and against F. D. Roosevelt with the alignments of the British political parties. True, some of the more hysterical opponents to the New Deal labelled it as 'creeping socialism' and saw Roosevelt as fundamentally hostile to the free enterprise economy. But it was the intention of the New Deal to rescue, not to destroy, American capitalism. Only by reducing words to the meaningless can the New Deal be regarded as socialist. If a Marxist (or Fascist) revolution was in the air, then the New Deal may have prevented it, but certainly did not lead it.

It is impossible to describe the New Deal by means of standard British party labels. It was in many respects more like Neville Chamberlain's attempt to bring the British economy in the 1930s under the shelter of his umbrella than the policies then advocated, or subsequently pursued, by the Labour Party; but it had many elements common to both, as also to the ideals of the nineteenth-century Liberal Party. If an attempt is made to represent the content of the New Deal in British terms, it would appear as a curiously coloured and oddly flavoured mixed economic cocktail of Lloyd George, Tom Mann, Montagu Norman, Ramsay Balderlain, unintentionally stirred with a mildly stimulating Keynesian swizzle-stick. But such a definition would leave out significant aspects of the New Deal which sprang from such wholly American phenomena as the populism of the 1890s and the progressivism of Theodore Roosevelt.

II POLITICAL ACHIEVEMENTS

This is not the place to discuss all the political aspects of the New Deal, but a few summary comments are necessary before we can proceed to economic analysis. F.D.R. was first and foremost a political animal and it was in the political arena that he won his greatest victories (by which it is not simply meant that his 1936 election victory was the largest for a century, or that he was the first and only American ever to be elected for three – and then for four – terms of office as President).

(i) Despite the catastrophic plight of the winter of 1933, Roosevelt led Americans away from the very real danger of revolution, or at least serious violence. The circumstances of his Inauguration were unique in American history : the nearest parallel, as the late Sir Denis Brogan once suggested, would have been Abraham Lincoln's Inauguration if the Civil War had just started the previous day. Roosevelt's words 'we do not distrust the future of social democracy' were among his most significant. The avoidance of major violence and bloodshed must be regarded as one of his greatest achievements.

(ii) F. D. Roosevelt used the office of President to convert the American public to an acceptance of the changed facts of economic life and of the need for fresh governmental attitudes. Seen as an exercise in public education, the New Deal succeeded in gaining general acceptance for the principle of the ultimate federal responsibility for the economic state of the nation. As observed earlier, despite the new technologies, many American nineteenth-century attitudes to economic life still lingered on in the 1920s. Some of these were destroyed in the Wall Street crash of 1929, but it was left to Roosevelt to inaugurate the American twentieth century politically by his proclamation of a general bank holiday on 9 March 1933, by which he demonstrated quite simply that the American President was in charge of the American economy. There has been no going back. The Nixon government, as much as the Johnson, Kennedy, Eisenhower and Truman governments before it, is committed to the doctrine that the federal government has the duty to regulate the economy, to prevent a depression and to achieve other economically desirable objectives. (Indeed present-day critics emphasise the allegedly excessive power of governmental bureaucracy, and in particular of the presidency, and have returned to the traditional American distrust of centralised and personalised power.) After Roosevelt the question ceased to be *whether* the federal government should intervene in the nation's economic life but became instead to what ends and by what means – new questions which in the long run are far more difficult to answer.

(iii) The role of the Supreme Court in economic affairs was

gradually re-defined. For the sort of economic measures needed in a modern society, an Executive impeded by the previously sound principles of division of power – above all in the need to have measures tested in the courts before they could be validated – was unable to act with requisite speed and authority. Since 1937 the Supreme Court has not invalidated any major piece of economic legislation, partly because the government learned as a result of New Deal experience to be more careful in its framing of legislation in order to avoid the judicial check.

This re-definition implied that the sphere of activity of inter-state commerce specifically granted to the federal government by the Constitution now came to be interpreted as embracing virtually all economic transactions. In other words, in the course of the 1930s, the American eighteenth-century Constitution was up-dated, in practice though not formally, to bring it into line with the realities of twentieth-century economic life. It was thus recognised that railroads had been built and gone into decline, that aeroplanes fly, that telegraph wires hum, or in other words that the political federation of the United States had at last become economically one nation.

In order to carry out the new extended functions of the federal government, it was necessary to build up a machinery of government where virtually none existed. During the course of the New Deal, the government recruited an administrative personnel of the sort needed to carry out its policies. Some of the 'bright young men' of the 1930s are still there. To their ranks have been added a never-ceasing flow of executives and bureaucrats at all levels. Despite American suspicions of 'professional' civil servants, non-elected and non-replaceable (again reflected today in feelings of impatience and impotence towards 'the system'), public service was raised 'above politics' in the 1930s to a far greater extent than ever before.

(iv) To establish these principles and set up this machinery required a hard-fought battle. As noted above, the American system of government always insisted on the written Constitution and on the formal separation of power. At the critical time when Roosevelt was groping towards an economic policy his attention was divided by political uncertainties.

By the end of the 1930s, however, there was no longer any serious question as to whether the government should intervene. It was a political achievement of the first magnitude that by the end of the

Roosevelt era the entanglements had been removed and all attention could thereafter be devoted instead to the question *how* and *to what purpose*.

III ECONOMIC EFFECTS OF THE NEW DEAL

If it is accepted that the main economic and social objectives of the New Deal were the three Rs – relief, recovery and reform – then it will serve as a useful framework for appraisal to examine its success in achieving each of these three purposes. As always it is the paramount duty of the economic historian, in examining consequences, in the first place to distinguish between the short run and the long run (and any intermediate 'runs' that may be appropriate); and in the second place to see beyond the obvious direct effects by probing into the indirect effects which often are far more important.

1 Relief

There can be no simple answer to the question of whether the New Deal achieved its object of providing relief. Clearly relief was made available, albeit patchily. Widespread famine did not occur. The death rate did not rise.

Whether or not the relief was adequate is a different matter. How should adequacy be measured? Compared with present-day social welfare provisions, the offerings were at best minimal, parsimonious and always subject to the Government's alarm at the cost of the relief payments.

This is perhaps a suitable place to repeat that distress in the United States was far more general than in Britain. All regions, states, economic groups, social classes, occupations and ages were liable to experience some degree of hardship. One major handicap under which the federal government worked was sheer ignorance, a simple lack of information about how many people were unemployed, and where, how great the suffering was and who the sufferers were. It had to rely on local informants, mainly voluntary social workers whose importance had been growing for a quarter of a century or more. Indeed, these were the people who focused attention both on the severity of the social problems and on the need for more information.

The existing arrangements for the relief of poverty in 1933 –

voluntary, semi-official and official – varied enormously from state to state, so that there was in some places a great deal to build upon, in others nothing. Since New Deal agencies, in the first place at any rate, relied on this existing corps of social workers both in the formulation and administration of policy, what could be done depended heavily on what already existed. The Federal Government relied on local social workers both to provide information on which to base its decisions and to provide personnel with which to implement them.

While the short-run effects of the relief measures were no more than palliative, in the long run they were of far-reaching significance. Relief granted as an expedient became relief granted as a principle, embodied in the Social Security Act of 1935 which formed the basis of all subsequent welfare legislation in the United States.

2 Recovery

The objective here was clear enough : to get the economy working 'normally' again, which implied a drastic reduction of unemployment together with a regular expansion of the national income and total employment.

The historical record set an ambitious target. For a century, and despite the fluctuations of the business cycle, the American gross national product had doubled every ten or fifteen years; it had displayed a prodigiously high labour-absorptive capacity (providing work in the 1900s, for example, for some 8 million immigrants *plus* the natural growth of the labour force, without any long-term increase in unemployment). 1933 was no time to define the targets too precisely, to ask (as we might today) what represented a minimum acceptable rate of economic expansion; with 20 per cent of the work force unemployed, it was even more academic to ask whether 1, 3 or 5 per cent unemployment represented the level compatible with a dynamic economy and a stable value of money. The only object was to get things going again and the only question was how this could be done.

To take an optimistic view of the New Deal one can argue, with A. M. Schlesinger Jr, that 'there was a swift recuperation of the American machine'. Every economic index hit rock-bottom in the winter of 1932–3. After Roosevelt's advent every year between 1933 and 1937 was better than its predecessor, no matter what statistics are examined. As was shown in the graph on p. 15, by 1937 the economy had been restored to the level of 1929.

Because recovery was incomplete, the magnitude of what was achieved should not be underestimated. The recovery of the years 1933–7 was almost as great as the expansion of 1922–9. If it is argued (as was done in Chapter 3) that the expansion of the twenties was indeed remarkable, then *ipso facto* a standard has already been set against which to measure the achievement of the thirties. And the simple observation is that the recovery of the thirties was about the same as the expansion of the twenties.

The extent of the recovery varied greatly in the different sectors of the economy. The broad picture is that the slowest response came in the investment sector, while recovery in the production of consumer goods was related generally to the durability of the product. Food, drink and tobacco production all rose quite sharply. The tobacco industry in particular experienced only a slight recession in 1932 and 1933; as early as 1934 cigarette output exceeded the 1928–9 level and by 1937 was nearly 40 per cent higher (and coffee imports incidentally followed a similar growth pattern). Richmond, Virginia – a centre of the tobacco industry with an economy well diversified in other directions – has claimed to have suffered less in the depression than any other city. Clothing production also rose quite sharply. Raw-cotton consumption in 1937 exceeded that of any previous year, but slumped rather badly in 1938. Raw-wool consumption surpassed its previous highest in 1935 and, apart from 1938, never again fell below the 1929 level. Rayon and acetate production continued to expand and by the mid-thirties was more than double that of the late twenties.

Automobile sales recovered more slowly, but in 1936 the number of passenger cars sold was about the same as the 1926–9 average and in 1937 exceeded that average. Car sales in 1937 were greater than in any previous year except 1929 and sales of trucks and buses the highest ever.

Yet, having observed these great improvements, we cannot conclude that they were sufficient. Merely to return to the level reached in 1928–9 did not amount to recovery. By no conceivable criteria can it be claimed that the years of Dr New Deal saw a complete restoration of the nation's economic health. The aggregate data set forward in Table 23 reveal the inadequacy of the recovery.

136

Table 23

Indexes of economic recovery, 1933–9

Year	G.N.P. (at constant prices)		Employment				Manufacturing	Investment		
	Total (1929=100)	Per capita (1929=100)	Total at work in millions	Employment index (1929=100)	Number of unemployed in millions	Unemployed as per cent of labour force	Production index (1929=100)	Total (1929=100)	As per cent of G.N.P.	Total new construction (1929=100)
1929	100	100	47.6	100	1.6	3	100	100	16	100
1933	69	67	38.8	81	12.8	25	63	9	3	27
1934	76	73	40.9	86	11.3	22	71	20	5	34
1935	83	80	42.3	89	10.6	20	82	40	9	39
1936	95	91	44.4	93	9.0	17	95	52	10	60
1937	100	94	46.3	97	7.7	14	105	73	13	65
1938	95	89	44.2	93	10.4	19	82	40	8	65
1939	103	96	45.8	96	9.5	17	100	57	10	76

These figures show that, although G.N.P. was about the same, over a million fewer persons were at work in 1937 than in 1929, while in 1939 a still smaller work force produced a slightly higher G.N.P. than in 1929. In manufacturing industries, for example, a similar output in 1939 was produced by half-a-million fewer workers than in 1929. In other words, while productivity continued to improve even during the depressed years, the total number of potentially employable persons grew from 49.2 million in 1929 to 54.0 million in 1937 and 55.2 million in 1939. The result was that the 1929 G.N.P. was achieved with an unemployment figure of $1\frac{1}{2}$ million while similar G.N.P. levels were reached in 1937 and 1939 with unemployment figures of over $7\frac{1}{2}$ million and $9\frac{1}{2}$ million respectively. The economy had lost its capacity to absorb additional labour.

One possible measure of the inadequacy of recovery is an estimate of what America's G.N.P. would have been in 1939 if unemployment had been at or near the 3 per cent level of 1929; or , to put the same point somewhat differently, what the G.N.P. would have been in 1939 if economic expansion had continued at the rate of the 1920s. There have been various estimates of this gap between actual and potential. The most dramatic of these has stated the shortfall to be approximately the same as the dollar cost to the United States of the Second World War (taking no account of the price of the depression in social distress).[1]

Two sets of data – employment and investment – dramatise the extent to which the undoubted improvement stopped far short of total recovery. The employment figures show that at no time in the 1930s were there as many people employed as at the peak of 1929 (46.3 million in 1937 compared with 47.6 million in 1929). The unemployment percentages were the most obvious index of the depression, never falling below 14 per cent. Even when allowance is made for statistical inaccuracies, there is little doubt that the *best* year of the 1930s (1937) had a higher unemployment percentage than the *worst* year of the 1920s (1922). By no stretch of the imagination can an economy with, at best, one in eight (14 per cent in 1937) of the labour force out of work be regarded as prosperous or even healthy.

The investment figures are even more significant. In the final analysis the depression was so severe and so prolonged because of the failure of investment to maintain, or even approach, its former level. Total annual investment in the 1930s never approximated to the \$16.2 billion of 1929; the nearest was \$11.8 billion in 1937. The failure of investment symbolised the complete collapse of confidence which was the ultimate psychological reason for America's plight. The New Deal succeeded neither in stimulating private investment nor in substituting for it public investment on a sufficient scale to set the economy on the road to recovery. At a generous estimate, *total* public works expenditure between 1933 and 1939 reached about \$12 billion, i.e. about three-quarters of the total private investment in the *one* year 1929.

A particularly good illustration is found in the continuing depression of the building-construction sector of the economy which had been so buoyant in the mid-1920s and so important an element in the high level of economic activity in that decade. Table 24 shows its fluctuation between 1929 and 1937.

TABLE 24

New construction activity, 1929–37

	Value (\$ billions)			(Total Index 1929 = 100)		
	1929	1933	1937	1929	1933	1937
Total new construction	10.8	2.9	7.0	100	27	65
New private construction	8.3	1.2	3.9	77	11	36
New public construction	2.5	1.6	3.1	23	15	29

Total construction had fallen by 1933 to about one-quarter of the 1929 level; private construction had slumped to one-seventh, but public construction was still two-thirds of the 1929 level. Between 1933 and 1937 private construction increased threefold, whereas public construction only doubled. The inadequacy of both is seen in the fact that total construction in 1937 was only two-thirds of the 1929 level; the inadequacy of the recovery of the private sector in particular is seen in the fact that in 1937 public construction had been raised to a level of about 25 per cent higher than that of 1929, whereas private construction was less than half. In 1929 new private construction was over three times greater than public, but in 1937 private exceeded public by a mere 25 per cent. To find a figure for total construction before 1927 lower than that of 1937 it is necessary to go back to 1921 ($6.0 billion); to find a lower value of private construction to 1918 ($2.9 billion). In this respect we find a sharp contrast with Britain, where building was far more active in the 1930s than in the 1920s and played a significant part in the recovery process.

IV ANALYSIS OF THE ECONOMIC FAILURE

As suggested earlier, the extent of the recovery during the mid-1930s should not be underestimated. Nor should the longer-term contributions of New Deal activities be overlooked, in particular the legacy of social capital created under the P.W.A. and W.P.A. (see above, p. 125) which proved of immense value during and after the Second World War.

Opponents of the New Deal, however, have always maintained that even the partial recovery came about despite, not because of, New Deal policies. To support this, they suggest that the first signs of recovery were visible as early as the summer of 1932, even before the November election. In the last five months of 1932, the *New York Times'* 'Weekly Index of Business Activity' (including production of steel, electricity and cars) rose by 11.5 per cent; this, it is argued, represented the beginning of a real recovery which was set back by the suspicions aroused by Roosevelt's campaign and election. In their turn, Roosevelt's supporters maintained that this improvement was an unreal one brought about for electoral reasons by the manipulations of Republican businessmen.

There would be more general agreement that the N.R.A. codes did more harm than good. They were a deterrent to expansion, raising costs, restricting output and in some cases directly discouraging new investment. Only after the Supreme Court's ruling against the N.R.A. in 1935 could real recovery get under way, and this is seen in the acceleration of the recovery process in the next two years.

It is clear that even in 1937 recovery was far from complete. The inadequacy of the public-works programme was compounded by the even greater failure to restore business confidence and, with it, enterprise and dynamism in the private sector of the economy. The only alternative was complete socialism; if, for whatever reasons, a government is not prepared to run the entire economy, then its prime task is to create conditions in which the private sector works, and works efficiently. The continuing depression resulted from the failure of investment caused not only by the loss of confidence resulting from the Wall Street collapse of 1929 but also from the inconsistencies of the New Deal itself.

Before we proceed to analyse further the causes of failure, a few preliminary observations are necessary.

(i) Political economy, even more than politics, is the art of the possible. Any government trying to influence economic conditions does not operate in a vacuum but in an extremely particular and concrete environment. That environment, which includes political institutions, existing pressure groups and public opinion, sets quite narrow limits to the range of practicable policies. Some of the inconsistencies in New Deal policies arose from the need to appease special interest groups primarily for non-economic, i.e. political or social, reasons. Even if economic theorists had themselves been able to suggest a clear-cut recovery programme, it is extremely doubtful if American politics and institutions in the mid-1930s would have allowed any government to persevere through thick and thin with the proposed remedies. In the pessimistic words of the Canadian economist, H. A. Innes, 'Democracy will beat the economist at every turn'.

(ii) The fact is, however, that the economists of the day did not and could not indicate to the American government what ought to be done. In the first place economic *statistics* were neither available rapidly enough nor on a sufficient scale in the 1930s to give the federal government an accurate picture of what exactly was going on in the economy. Correct and up-to-date information must be the starting-point for any sort of policy-making; vague general impressions are not enough, particularly in a country as big as America, with widely diverse problems from one region to another. The New Deal itself did much to improve this situation through the many fact-finding agencies which it set up and which eventually came to provide much essential data for national policy-making. Yet another New Deal legacy of great benefit to post-war America has been the quantity, quality and immediacy of economic statistics.

In the second place economic *theory* in the 1930s had no solution to offer. Keynesian economics were only just being propounded and were not generally accepted. Roosevelt himself was no economist, and retained to the end an orthodox general belief in the balanced budget. Keynes himself was a great admirer of Roosevelt, anxious that he should succeed, alarmed by the possible consequences if he failed. He supported F.D.R.'s withdrawal from the World Economic Conference in 1933, agreeing that salvation was not to be found in a general return to a Gold Standard. Although a small number of Roosevelt's advisers were influenced by the development of Keynesian economics in the 1930s, the majority were not, including such important reasons as Henry Morgenthau Jr, Roosevelt's Secretary of the Treasury.

As seen earlier, there is still no consensus of opinion among economists about the causes of the severity and the duration of the American depression of the 1930s; the diagnoses are conflicting, even contradictory. For people living through those years – and faced with countless urgent decisions to be taken – it was even more difficult to analyse what had gone wrong, and to be sure enough about their diagnosis to be able to prescribe definite remedies and to apply those remedies whatever opposition was aroused.

V FISCAL POLICY

The main policy prescription for an economy in depression, made explicit by John Maynard Keynes in *The General Theory of Employment, Interest and Money* (1936), was deficit spending. Keynes condemned the balanced budget as inappropriate to depression conditions, advocating instead that governments should stimulate recovery by deliberately spending not within but beyond their means, i.e. by reacting to falling revenues, not by curtailing expenditure or by increasing taxes, but by increasing expenditure still further and, if anything, reducing taxes.

As observed earlier, Roosevelt promised in the 1932 election to balance the federal budget and he did not abandon this aim. In the event, the Government never succeeded in balancing the federal finances. The deficits however were unintentional, resulting from the failure of avowed government policy, not its achievement. When the deficit reached $4½ million in 1936, the Government began a severe curtailment of expenditure in 1937, and this was at least a contributory cause of the recession of 1938.

Roosevelt was assailed by contemporaries for his failure to balance expenditure and revenue. Subsequent writers have placed a different interpretation on the events, seeing in the failure of the New Deal to stimulate recovery a failure to use fiscal policy as a means to recovery. Table 25 presents the balance-sheet.

TABLE 25

Federal income and expenditure, 1929–39

	Federal expenditure in billion dollars	Federal revenue in billion dollars	Balance in billion dollars	G.N.P. in billion dollars (current)	Federal expenditure as % G.N.P.	Federal revenue as % G.N.P.
1929	3.3	4.0	+ 0.7	104	3.2	3.9
1930	3.4	4.2	+ 0.7	91	3.8	4.6
1931	3.6	3.1	− 0.5	76	4.7	4.1
1932	4.7	1.9	− 2.7	59	8.0	3.3
1933	4.6	2.0	− 2.6	56	8.3	3.6
1934	6.7	3.1	− 3.6	65	10.3	4.7
1935	6.5	3.7	− 2.8	73	9.0	5.1
1936	8.5	4.1	− 4.4	83	10.3	4.9
1937	7.8	5.0	− 2.8	91	8.5	5.5
1938	6.8	5.6	− 1.2	85	8.0	6.6
1939	8.9	5.0	− 3.9	91	9.7	5.5
1946	61.7	43.5	− 18.2	211	29.6	20.7
1970	196.6	193.7	− 2.9	977	20.1	19.8

SOURCE: Tables 25 and 26 have been compiled from *Historical Statistics* and recent *Economic Reports of the President*. Discrepancies occur in the published figures, but those given here are as accurate and consistent as possible.

The following points emerge from Table 25 :

(i) Total federal expenditure (Col. 1) increased in most years from 1929 to 1936. Nevertheless, total expenditure in the peak years (1936 and 1939) was less than double the 1932 Hoover figure; as a percentage of G.N.P. (Col. 5) the difference was between 8.0 per cent in 1932 and 10.3 per cent in 1936. The main increases occurred, as would be expected, in aid to agriculture, relief and work-relief, and public works. On these items total expenditure grew from $1.0 billion in 1933 to $4.0 billion in 1936 (and at peak, $4.8 billion in 1939).

(ii) The federal deficit (Col. 3) did not increase regularly, although the deficits in 1934, 1935, 1936, 1937 and 1939 all exceeded that of 1932. The deficit was drastically reduced in 1937 and 1938, but increased again in 1939. The greatest deficit (1936) was considerably short of double that of 1932, a difference of degree rather than a fundamental departure in policy. Nevertheless the case must not be overstated. The argument is not that the fiscal activity of the federal government gave no stimulus at all, but that it did not give enough. Until the sharp cut-back in expenditure between 1937 and 1938, seen in the considerably reduced deficit in 1938 (and reflected in the sharp recession of that year), the effects of federal fiscal actions were expansionary through the mid-1930s.

(iii) Total revenue (Col. 2) grew annually between 1933 and 1938. This was in part a direct consequence of the recovery itself (for the same reason that revenue fell between 1930 and 1932). But no attempt was made to stimulate expenditure through tax reduction; when any change was made this was to increase, rather than lower, the effective rate of taxation. Column 6 shows that the federal government was collecting in taxes a steadily growing percentage of the G.N.P. through these years, reaching 6.6 per cent in 1938, almost double the 1929 percentage. It will be observed that receipts from income tax and corporation tax both increased from 1933 to 1938.

TABLE 26

Sources of federal revenue, 1929–39

	Income-tax	Corpora-tion tax	Excise Taxes (in billion dollars)	Customs	Other (inc. estate taxes)	Total
1929	1.1	1.2	0.5	0.6	0.6	4.0
1932	0.4	0.6	0.5	0.3	0.1	1.9
1933	0.4	0.4	0.8	0.3	0.1	2.0
1934	0.4	0.4	1.3	0.3	0.7	3.1
1935	0.5	0.6	1.4	0.3	0.9	3.7
1936	0.7	0.8	1.5	0.4	0.7	4.1
1937	1.1	1.1	1.8	0.5	0.5	5.0
1938	1.3	1.3	1.7	0.4	0.9	5.6
1939	1.0	1.2	1.8	0.3	0.7	5.0

The full story of the income-tax needs to be traced back to the 1920s. As observed in Chapter 2, a permanent income-tax had been introduced as recently as 1913. After several increases during the First World War the policy of the governments of the 1920s, in keeping with the economic philosophy of the day and the desire to return to pre-war 'normalcy', had been to reduce sharply the incidence of income-tax – a trend which reached the lowest point following the Budget of 1927.

The Budget which set the stage for the 1930s was the ill-conceived Revenue Act of 1932. In the face of declining federal revenues, the Hoover Government had reacted to the deepening gloom of the depression in a Budget which, instead of decreasing the tax burden in order to stimulate private expenditure, greatly increased tax rates. The Revenue Act of 1932 not only raised sharply both standard and surtax rates, but also lowered personal exemptions. The results can be seen in the effective tax rates shown in Table 27. The New Deal Budgets continued to aim at a balance, seeking to offset the greater expenditures by raising more revenue, and tax rates were only slightly reduced as yields began to rise with the improvement in incomes. Moreover, social justice seemed to require a higher tax burden to be placed on the wealthier members of society, and social policy was given priority over economic policy with the raising of surtax rates in 1935.

TABLE 27

Effective rate (per cent) of U.S. income-tax

| | | | on incomes of | | |
	$5000	$10,000	$20,000	$50,000	$100,000
1923	1.0	3.4	6.2	12.9	22.6
1926	0.2	0.8	2.9	9.7	16.0
1929	0.1	0.4	2.4	8.3	14.8
1932	1.4	4.2	8.1	17.1	30.0
1934	1.0	3.4	7.3	17.2	30.2
1936	1.0	3.4	7.3	17.2	32.0

Thus at all levels of income over $5000 (the minimum), the incidence of income-tax was higher throughout the depressed thirties than during the prosperous twenties, the very reverse of Keynesian counter-cyclical fiscal policy.

(iv) The discussion still lacks a further important dimension. We must remind ourselves that in addition to the federal government, there were forty-eight separate state governments and hundreds of local governments. The respective shares of total taxation raised by the different governmental bodies are given in Table 28.

TABLE 28

Share of total taxation raised by different governments

	Federal *(per cent)*	State *(per cent)*	Local *(per cent)*
1927	36	17	47
1932	23	24	54
1934	33	23	44
1936	37	25	39
1938	41	24	35

While it was argued earlier that the effects of federal fiscal activity were mildly expansionary, those of state and local governments certainly operated in the opposite direction. State and local governments were even more anxious than the Federal Government not to spend beyond their means and tried to hold expenditure down while maintaining or improving their incomes. The *total* sum raised in taxation by governments at all three levels was over 50 per cent higher in 1938 than in 1932 ($12.9 billion compared with $8.0 billion). In an important article, E. Cary Brown[2] reached the conclusion that in most years the mild expansiveness of federal fiscal actions did no more than counter the contractive effects of state and local actions, and that between 1933 and 1939 the total impact of fiscal actions was counter-inflationary, i.e. restrictive rather than expansionary. Brown attributes this primarily to the general increase in taxation at all levels of government. Nevertheless, there is a danger in drawing conclusions from the *aggregate* figures of state and local finance; it does not necessarily follow that the effect was similar in all areas, and before final verdicts can be passed it would be necessary to have a detailed fiscal balance-sheet for taxes raised and moneys spent by all three governments for the separate regions, and preferably for each separate state.

The set-back involved in the thirteen-month contraction from May 1937 to June 1938 was an important turning-point. Its severity can hardly be exaggerated. It was one of the sharpest declines in all American experience, with a 2 million drop in total employment, an increase of at least one-third in the already high figure of unemployment, a 30 per cent fall in industrial output, and even more of durable-goods production, and a 45 per cent curtailment of total investment.

But it was also as a result of this experience that enough members of the Administration realised the mistake of cutting down expenditure in 1937 and, either empirically or theoretically, at last accepted the necessity of deficit spending. Belatedly in the spring of 1938 great increases in expenditure were authorised and by the summer these were already providing a new stimulus to recovery.

VI MONETARY POLICY

Monetary policy paralleled fiscal policy so closely in this period that it is usually regarded as having been largely subservient to the dictates of the Treasury, particularly to the desire of the latter to minimise the cost of its own borrowing by keeping inerest rates as low and stable as possible. Until 1936 there was a mildly inflationary expansion of the currency; thereafter, at the time of the curtailment of federal expenditure, the Federal Reserve System also took steps which were interpreted as intentionally deflationary. Thus fiscal and monetary measures both helped to precipitate the decline of 1937–8.

After America's abandonment of the Gold Standard in April 1933, the dollar was devalued in gold terms. All gold holdings were centralised in the Treasury (to prevent hoarding and in an effort to restore faith in the paper currency); on 1 February 1934 the price of gold was fixed at $35 per fine-ounce (at which it remained until 1972), the Treasury undertaking to buy at that rate all gold presented to it.

The growing political tensions in Europe in the mid-1930s resulted in a large repatriation of American loans. These withdrawals both aggravated the international problem of illiquidity and helped to bring about a massive shift of gold from Europe to the United States (assisted also by the fact that America continued to import less than she exported and thus had a surplus in her balance of visible trade). Some $10 billion of gold moved into the United States between 1934 and 1939. The Treasury's gold stock approximately quadrupled but, as in the twenties, the gold accumulation was not allowed to induce a major expansion of the currency. Some of the gold did find its way into the domestic economy, however, and greatly increased total bank reserves, and the amount of currency in circulation was 20 per cent greater in 1937 than in 1934.

The inflationary potential of the growing bank reserves alarmed the Federal Reserve Board (quite unnecessarily, it would appear in retrospect). Armed with the new powers granted to it in the Banking Act of 1935, to change reserve ratios, the System raised the required ratios in August 1936 and again in March and May of 1937. These actions had the intended effect of reducing effective bank reserves, but were interpreted by the banking and business communities as announcing a need for frugality. Thus, even though the economy was still very far from full employment, these monetary measures combined with the fiscal retrenchment to put into reverse the economic advance of the previous four years, and must be regarded as powerful contributory causes of the calamitous and unnecessary contraction of 1937–8.

In passing any final judgement on the success of the New Deal's economic policies it has to be borne in mind that the expansive momentum achieved by 1936 was impressive. Had that progress been maintained, the economic situation in 1939 would have been very different; unemployment, for example, could very well have fallen to below 5 million and thus have been no more than half the 17 per cent actually recorded.

It is self-evident that America's economic problems were not solved until long after the outbreak of war in Europe. Unemployment remained above 10 per cent until the middle of 1941. At this point the whole pattern of government expenditure changed drastically, increasing from $8.8 billion in 1939 to $34 billion in 1942 and $80 billion in 1943, while war production entirely transformed the private sector of the economy.

If the discussion above leads to the conclusion that the New Deal failed to achieve its economic purposes, an examination of its reform measures may lead to a more favourable verdict. The policy expedients were inappropriate and inadequate to solve the immediate and serious economic problems, but the measures taken during the mid-thirties to remedy the institutional weaknesses, and to change social attitudes and relationships, were as important as any in the nation's history. Indeed it is arguable that no other years except the 1790s saw such a concentration of fundamental decisions affecting American society. To conclude this assessment of the achievement of the New Deal, we must examine briefly the main reforms which were introduced.

1   Banking

The measures taken in the Glass–Steagall Banking Reform Act of 1933 (see above, p. 117) were carried further in the Banking Act of 1935. These two Acts between them restored the possibility of a central supervision of America's money and banking practices which had been destroyed almost exactly a century earlier when President Andrew Jackson refused to re-charter the Second Bank of the United States. Until the reform of the Federal Reserve System by these two Acts, the United States lacked any central banking authority.

The Federal Reserve System, although set up in 1913, had so far failed to provide a flexible currency and banking stability, or to prevent runs on the banks. The two New Deal Banking Acts provided the System with more appropriate instruments with which to achieve these objects. In addition to the new authority given to the 'Fed' in 1933, the following new provisions were made in 1935 :

(i) The Board of Governors was reconstituted in order to achieve better co-ordination among the member banks. The Treasury was no longer to be represented on the Board.

(ii) The Board was given permanent authority, without the previous need for presidential approval, to vary required reserve ratios in either direction; the country-bank ratio of 7 : 1, the reserve-city-bank ratio of 10 : 1 and the central-reserve-city-bank ratio of 13 : 1 could all be doubled.

(iii) The so-called 'Regulation Q' was also made permanent. This enabled the 'Fed' to regulate the rate of interest on deposits.

(iv) The Federal Open Market Committee, eventually to become a major instrument of monetary control, was established.

It is, however, one thing to provide instruments for carrying out policies, another to decide on correct policies. When a central monetary authority makes a mistake, the outcome can be far more serious than if there is no such authority. As already observed, the first use by the 'Fed' of its new powers, its raising of reserve requirements in 1936–7, was inappropriate and harmful. Similarly, the reconstitution of the Board without Treasury representation did not immediately strengthen its independence since the Treasury still retained its control over the management of the National Debt.

Nevertheless, the new powers given to the Board (together with new theoretical developments in the field of monetary economics) set the scene for the much more successful (some would say extremely successful) use of monetary policy in the United States since 1945.

2 Business operations

Even if the behaviour of the Stock Exchange did not in itself cause the instability of the late 1920s, the spectacle of the Wall Street collapse had focused attention on the conduct of its business. The establishment of the S.E.C. (see above, pp. 125–6) must be regarded as a major New Deal reform and one of the most successful. The mere suppression of undesirable practices may appear a purely negative achievement, yet the enhanced stability of, and confidence in, the stock market has been an extremely important factor in the post-war years. While many would argue over details, few would challenge the view that the S.E.C. has exercised a salutary control over stock dealings during a period characterised for the most part by great activity and expansion. When one presidential candidate in 1968 so much as mentioned the possibility that the S.E.C. might have outstayed its welcome, the reaction from all sides was such that he never returned to the subject again.

In another sphere of business regulation the late 1930s saw a change of direction in policy that can be regarded as a measure of reform. It was observed earlier that the Blue Eagle policy of the N.R.A. had in effect set the anti-trust policy of the Sherman and

Clayton Acts in abeyance. After a period of uncertainty following the invalidation of the N.R.A. in the Schechter Case (see pp. 169–70), the appointment in 1938 of Thurman Arnold as Assistant Attorney-General in charge of the anti-trust division of the Justice Department heralded a new burgeoning of anti-trust activity.[3] Although Arnold had implied in his book *The Folklore of Capitalism* that industrial combinations were a social necessity and anti-trust laws a ritual, but intentionally ineffective, mode of condemnation, he soon proved to be the most energetic trust-buster since the passage of the Sherman Act. Within five years he had instituted almost as many anti-monopoly actions as in the previous fifty, attacking restrictive patents and monopolistic practices by both unions and business, and taking on such giants as General Electric and the Aluminum Company of America. Arnold's campaign, if vigorous, however, can hardly be adjudged successful, partly because, as in 1917, the advent of the Second World War once more turned nefarious collusion into laudable co-operation. Like so much of the New Deal, Thurman Arnold's legacy is to be found in institutional improvement rather than practical effects; he greatly enlarged the personnel of the anti-trust division and transformed it into a fighting force, well prepared for the battles that lay ahead after 1945.

3 Agriculture

To stand aside from the details and contradictions of New Deal agricultural policy and ask whether and how agriculture benefited in the long run from the experiments of the 1930s is not an easy task. Agriculture presented the classic New Deal dilemma : whether to pursue the socially desirable policy of relieving poverty wherever it existed or the economically desirable policy of reducing the number of producers; and which policy to choose when social and economic criteria came into conflict. The problems were further confused by the complexity and diversity of American agriculture. Some farmers were in trouble because they belonged to a permanently depressed 'submerged third' in American agriculture (and since many of these were black sharecroppers in the South, the ingredient of colour was added to the mixture). Others faced difficulties because they were producing the wrong crops and could not, or would not, change or diversify, or because their earlier farming methods had ruined the land on which they depended. Some were viable farmers but had now become direct victims of the depression; others suffered from the malignancy of Nature during the 1930s.

It would generally be agreed that the A.A.A. of 1933 did little or nothing to help those at the very bottom of the heap; indeed acreage reduction sometimes led to the eviction of the least secure tenant-farmers, including some 350,000 Southern sharecroppers over half of whom were black. Over the decade farm employment contracted by 1½ million (suggesting that, whatever the intention of policy, the outcome was in the direction of an 'economic' rather than a 'social' solution).

The main benefits accrued to the better-off farmers, who in general needed help the least but whose larger units made mechanisation and more scientific farming possible (see Table 5, p. 29). We probably have to conclude that the most lasting New Deal legacy in agriculture was, paradoxically, improved efficiency. A massive programme of education greatly reduced soil erosion, began to teach contour ploughing, dry farming and the rationalisation of crops; programmes for conservation and land rehabilitation, irrigation, reservoir building, not to mention experiments in co-operative activities and regional planning, all helped to bring about a more soundly based agriculture for the war and post-war period (though at some cost in the increase of what has been described as 'the heavy hand of bureaucratic paternalism and technological determinism').[4]

If reform in agriculture was largely on the side of improved efficiency and the elimination of the weak, it should also be recognised that with the Agricultural Adjustment Act of 1938 a fresh and more intelligent approach was being made to the perennial problem of over-production.

4 Labour

The extravagant claim has been made that the transformation in the situation of organised labour in the 1930s was a social revolution comparable to the freeing of the slaves. There can be no doubt of the dramatic change in power relationships that followed the legalisation of trade unions by the Wagner Act and the subsequent rapid growth of industrial unionism. In 1930 about 10 per cent of the non-agricultural work force was unionised; by 1939 over half of all industrial workers were in trade unions. Organised labour had indeed become a power in the land.

It would be a mistake to assume that this development resulted from deliberate policies pursued by President Roosevelt. His election in 1932 owed little or nothing to trade union support; several important unionists were Republicans and supported Hoover. The evidence suggests that Roosevelt subsequently acquiesced in rather than inaugurated the new labour policy. What political leadership there was came from individual members of Congress, above all Robert F. Wagner and Robert La Follette Jr, and from Roosevelt's Secretary of Labor, Frances Perkins. It is not to underestimate their contribution to insist that the main dynamism nevertheless came from within the ranks of labour itself, and above all from that towering personality, John L. Lewis. Building upon the spontaneous growth already clearly visible in the early 1930s, in such industries as the automobile industry, the carefully devised strategy for unionising unskilled workers depended on meticulous planning and massive organisation. The aim was legal status, not immediate industrial benefit, i.e. to force the big corporations to accept the new position of unions in the eyes of the law by granting them recognition and agreeing to collective bargaining. The automobile, steel and coal industries were selected and the main weapon of attack was the sit-in strike. The crucial victory followed the sit-down occupation of the General Motors Plant at Flint, Michigan, at the beginning of 1937; once the newly elected Governor of Michigan, Frank Murphy, had refused to intervene, General Motors recognised the United Automobile Workers (U.A.W.) in February 1937 and union recognition by the U.S. Steel Corporation soon followed. Ford Motors capitulated in 1940 and the other steel firms on America's entry into the war. Union membership rose from 3.2 million in 1932 and 3.7 million in 1935 to 8.3 million in 1938, 8.9 million in 1940 and 13.6 million in 1943. This vast increase in union membership was facilitated by an institutional change as far-reaching as the legal change. In 1935 the Committee for Industrial Organization, with John L. Lewis as president, was constituted out of eight industrial unions within the A.F. of L. In 1938 this group consolidated its existence as a separate body, the Congress of Industrial Organization. The means were now available for the unionisation of American unskilled industrial workers.

'A week', Mr Harold Wilson once said, 'is a long time in politics.' 'A year', one might add, 'is a short time in economics.' Much of the conflict arising from attempts of governments to influence economic conditions derives from the tensions implicit in these comments. Economic change takes a long time, often a very long time, to work out; things do not happen at a stroke. To the extent that politicians, and electorates, expect quick results, many types of economic intervention are doomed to frustration if not complete failure. Forward planning in economic life has a time-horizon of years, in some cases decades. Many measures may have an immediate and direct impact, like the plop of a stone thrown into the middle of a pond, but their full effects, like the subsequent ripples, continue to work their way slowly into every corner long after the original first shock. If the effects of New Deal measures have one single lesson to teach it is surely that the indirect effects of government intervention, often unforeseen and unintended, may in the long run be the most important; the more complex and interwoven an economy, the more complicated and distant the final results. This is not necessarily a counsel of despair, but is certainly one of caution : not to expect governments to be able to work economic miracles, since the total performance of the economy sets the ultimate limits of the possible; and not to assume simplistic causal relationships between steps taken and immediate, uncomplicated consequences.

A successful economic policy, argues the Swedish economist Erik Lundberg,[5] requires three essential ingredients : a precise (not a vague) formulation of ends; a choice of means appropriate to the achievement of those ends, without the means themselves being allowed to take on the character of ends (e.g. tax increases or reductions regarded as ends in themselves, not as instruments of policy); and the avoidance of undesirable indirect consequences from any measures taken. These three ingredients are likely to be present only if the starting-point is full information about, and theoretical understanding of, the workings of the economic system. The New Deal did not fulfil any of these criteria. The knowledge and understanding which the policy-makers had of American conditions at the time were quite inadequate. The aims themselves were imprecise, the means adopted inconsistent and inappropriate for the achievement of those aims, and the subsequent indirect effects often quite unforeseen. It is perhaps not altogether surprising that these incidental and unintended consequences of the New Deal turned out in the long run to be the most important.

The foregoing survey has suggested that the New Deal failed in its most important single task of restoring economic prosperity to the United States. The contrast with Britain is instructive. Britain's economic recovery in the thirties had a sounder basis and went considerably further than America's, not because of government measures but because longer-term forces were at work. The areas of growth to which Britain could turn in the thirties – building, electrification and the motor-car industry – were precisely those on which America's expansion in the twenties had depended, and represented the beginning of a catching-up process. For the reasons examined earlier, these areas offered no further potential for growth in the United States. To be sure, there were in both countries a number of latent 'new' industries, but these did not in themselves provide a sufficient impetus for major advance.

We are left with a picture of America in the 1930s which must be extremely confused, in which paradoxes, ironies and contradictions abound, and include a curious blend of continuity and uniqueness. By 1929 the American economy had reached a point where it could no longer follow its former lines of development under its traditional assumptions. Public opinion, a very intangible concept in the United States, had to be educated to an acceptance of the necessity of a thorough readjustment of economic institutions, practices and attitudes (as much as is needed in Britain in 1974). The problems of adjustment were too great to be solved by the expedients of the New Deal. But by the end of the thirties sufficient progress had been made towards creating new environmental and institutional conditions that longer-term solutions of the problem became possible. Not all American precedents were irrelevant, even in the thirties. There is some significance in the fact that, while the British government provided doles, the American government supplied jobs. The old belief in salvation through hard work remained powerful, and salutary. The provision of work greatly helped the process of vindicating America's self-respect. Despite the greater severity of the depression in America than in Britain, the scars healed more quickly over there and post-war, and present-day economic problems have been and are easier to handle because of the much less acrid legacy of hatred from those years.

Chronology of Events

1917   6 Apr.   United States enters First World War.

1918   11 Nov.   The Armistice.

      12 Dec.   President Woodrow Wilson leaves for Paris Peace Conference.

      23 Dec.   All food controls suspended.

1919   1 Jan.   War Industries Board disbanded.

      6 Jan.   Death of ex-President Theodore Roosevelt.

      22 Sept.   Strike starts at U.S. Steel, Gary, Indiana. First of several major strikes.

      26 Sept.   Start of President Wilson's illness.

      28 Oct.   Prohibition Enforcement Act (Volstead Amendment) passed by Congress over President's Veto. Prohibition from 16 January 1920 of all beverages with over 0.5 per cent alcohol.

      19 Nov.   Versailles Treaty fails to receive two-thirds majority in Senate. Voting: for 53; against 38.

      24 Dec.   Railroads returned to private ownership, from 1 March 1920.

1920   16 Jan.   Prohibition goes into effect.

      1 Mar.   U.S. *v.* U.S. Steel Corporation case. Supreme Court decides U.S.S.C. *not* an illegal monopoly.

      19 Mar.   Senate again refuses to ratify Versailles Treaty.

      26 Aug.   Nineteenth Amendment (Woman Suffrage) proclaimed.

      2 Nov.   Presidential Election: Warren G. Harding (Rep.) 16.2 million votes, James M. Cox (Dem.) 9.1 million votes; Eugene V. Debs (Socialist) 0.9 million votes. Republican vice-presidential candidate, Calvin Coolidge; Democratic vice-presidential candidate, Franklin D. Roosevelt.

1921	4 Mar.	Inauguration of President WARREN G. HARDING and Vice-President Calvin Coolidge. Cabinet includes A. W. Mellon (Sec. of Treasury); Henry C. Wallace (Agriculture); Herbert C. Hoover (Commerce); Will H. Hays (P.M.G.).
	19 May	First Immigration Quota Act restricting immigration to 3 per cent of nationality living in the United States in 1910.
	26 Sept.	Unemployment Conference in Washington (Hoover Chairman); about $3\frac{1}{2}$ million unemployed.
1922	19 Sept.	Fordney–McCumber Tariff Act. Highest-ever import duties.
1923	2 Aug.	Death of President Harding.
	3 Aug.	CALVIN COOLIDGE sworn in as President.
1924	16 Jan.	McNary–Haugen Farm Relief Bill fails to pass Congress. (Failed again in 1926; passed in 1928 but vetoed by President Coolidge.)
	3 Feb.	Death of Woodrow Wilson.
	26 May	Second Immigration Quota Act. 2 per cent of numbers resident in the United States in 1890. (Went into effect 1 July 1929.)
	2 June	Revenue Act reduces surtax, estate and income-taxes; most excise taxes abolished.
	16 Aug.	Dawes Plan for payment of German reparations agreed.
	19 Dec.	William Green succeeds Samuel Gompers as President of the A.F. of L.
1925	4 Mar.	CALVIN COOLIDGE inaugurated as President (after election previous November): V.-P. Charles G. Dawes. Cabinet includes F. B. Kellogg (Secretary of State), Mellon (Treasury), Hoover (Commerce).
	26 July	Death of W. J. Bryan.
1926	26 Feb.	Revenue Act further reduces income-tax, surtax and estate tax.

25 May	Public Buildings Act authorises expenditure of $165 million on federal buildings.
25 Sept.	8-hour day and 5-day week introduced by Ford Motor Company.
2 Nov.	Robert La Follette jr. (Rep. Wisc.) elec. to Senate.

1927	7 Jan.	Opening of New York–London radio-telephone service.
	Apr.	4 million acres of Mississippi Valley flooded.
	7 Apr.	Herbert Hoover (in Washington) televised in New York.
	20–21 May	Charles A. Lindbergh's non-stop solo trans-Atlantic flight.
	26 May	15-millionth Ford motor-car.
	12 Nov.	Holland Tunnel (under Hudson River, N.Y.) opened.
	Dec.	Ford Model A car put on show.

1928	15 May	Flood Control Act authorises expenditure of $325 million on lower Mississippi.
	25 May	Muscle Shoals Bill (for construction of hydro-electricity plant on Tennessee River) passed by Congress but 'pocket-vetoed' by Coolidge.
	6 Nov.	Herbert Hoover (Rep.) elected President, with 21.4 million votes over Alfred E. Smith (Dem.) with 15.0 million votes. Franklin Delano Roosevelt (Dem.) elected Governor of New York State.
	21 Dec.	Act passed for building of Boulder Dam.

1929	2 Feb.	Federal Reserve Board forbids member banks to make loans for stock speculation on margin.
	4 Mar.	HERBERT HOOVER inaugurated President. V.-P. Charles Curtis. Cabinet includes: Henry L. Stimson (Secretary of State), Mellon (Treasury).
	15 June	Agricultural Marketing Act. $500 million provided for advisory Federal Farm Board.
	23 Oct.	Minor panic on N.Y. Stock Exchange.
	24 Oct.	Major panic. 19 million shares change hands.
	29 Oct.	Collapse of New York Stock Market.

	21 Nov.	Hoover's conference with representatives of big business.
	2 Dec.	Ford Motor Company increases minimum wage from $6 to $7 per day.
1930	31 Mar.	Public Buildings Act increases appropriation of Act of 1926 by $230 million.
	4 Apr.	Congressional appropriation of $300 million to continue federal aid to state road building.
	17 June	Hoover signs Hawley–Smoot Tariff Bill raising tariffs still higher.
	Aug.	Serious drought in Mid-west and South.
	17 Sept.	Work begun on Hoover Dam (completed 1936).
	2 Dec.	Hoover's annual presidential message to Congress requests $100 to $150 million for construction of public works ($116 million authorised on 20 December).
	11 Dec.	Failure of Bank of the United States in New York City.
1931	3 Mar.	Muscle Shoals Bill vetoed by President Hoover.
	1 May	Empire State Building (N.Y.C.) completed.
	21 Sept.	Britain leaves Gold Standard.
	24 Oct.	George Washington Bridge (N.Y.C.) opened.
	8 Dec.	Hoover's annual message proposes Emergency Reconstruction Finance Corporation and Public Works Administration.
1932	12 Jan.	First woman Senator elected (for Arkansas).
	22 Jan.	Reconstruction Finance Corporation authorised by Congress.
	7 Mar.	Congress authorises distribution through Red Cross of 45 million bushels of wheat.
	23 Mar.	Norris–La Guardia Act signed by President Hoover.
	17 June	Putnam Bonus Bill rejected by Senate. Bonus Army of 11,000 veterans camped near Washington D.C.
	2 July	Franklin Delano Roosevelt accepts Democratic nomination as presidential candidate and pledges 'a new deal for the American people'.

21 July	British Imperial Economic Conference meets in Ottawa, partly in response to Hawley–Smoot Tariff.
21 July	Emergency Relief and Construction Act empowers R.F.C. to lend $1.8 billion to states for relief and public works.
22 July	Home Loan Bank Act.
28 July	Bonus Army driven out of Washington by General Douglas A. MacArthur.
26 Aug.	Moratorium on first-mortgage foreclosures.
17 Oct.	Al Capone sentenced to 11 years' imprisonment for income-tax evasion.
25 Oct.	Conference in Washington ends with statement by Hoover and French Premier Laval promising maintenance of the Gold Standard in the United States and France.
31 Oct.	12-day bank holiday proclaimed in Nevada.
8 Nov.	F. D. Roosevelt (Dem.) elected President with 22.8 million votes; Hoover (Rep.) 15.8 million votes.

1933	13 Feb.	8-day bank holiday proclaimed in Michigan. Numerous other States follow suit.
	20 Feb.	Repeal of Prohibition (21st Amendment).
	4 Mar.	Governor of New York declares bank holiday.
The Hundred Days	4 Mar.	Inauguration of FRANKLIN D. ROOSEVELT as President. V.-P., John N. Garner (Texas). Cabinet includes: Cordell Hull (Secretary of State), Harold L. Ickes (Interior), Henry A. Wallace (Agriculture), Frances Perkins (Labor).
	5 Mar.	Roosevelt proclaims national bank holiday and embargo on gold exportation.
	9 Mar.	Emergency Banking Act.
	13 Mar.	Banks begin to re-open.
	20 Mar.	Economy Act.
	31 Mar.	C.C.C. created by Unemployment Relief Act.
	19 Apr.	America leaves Gold Standard.
	12 May	F.E.R.A. set up by Federal Emergency Relief Act.
	12 May	A.A.A. set up by Agricultural Adjustment Act.

12 May	Emergency Farm Mortgage Act.
18 May	T.V.A. set up by Tennessee Valley Authority Act.
5 June	Abrogation of gold clause in public and private contracts.
12 June	World Monetary and Economic Conference convenes in London.
13 June	H.O.L.C. set up by Home Owners' Refinancing Act.
16 June	F.C.A. set up by Farm Credit Act.
16 June	N.R.A. and P.W.A. set up by National Industrial Recovery Act.
16 June	Glass–Steagall Banking Reform Act.
16 June	Federal Coordination of Transport set up by Railroad Coordination Act.

3 July	America rejects currency stabilisation plan drawn up by London Conference. Conference wound up 27 July.
5 Aug.	N.L.B. set up under the N.R.A.
25 Oct.	Devaluation of dollar to 66 cents gold. R.F.C. authorised to purchase newly mined gold at $31.36 per oz.
7 Nov.	Fiorello H. La Guardia elected mayor of New York City.
9 Nov.	C.W.A. set up by executive order.
5 Dec.	Repeal of Prohibition goes into effect.

1934	31 Jan.	Dollar fixed at 59.06 cents gold value.
	31 Jan.	F.F.M.C. created by Farm Mortgage Refinancing Act.
	10 May	Dust storm in Texas, Oklahoma, Kansas and Colorado.
	6 June	S.E.C. set up by Act of Congress.
	12 June	Reciprocal Trade Agreements Act.
	19 June	N.L.B. of 1933 replaced by N.L.R.B.
	19 June	F.C.C. set up to supervise telephone, telegraph and radio.
	28 June	F.H.A. set up by National Housing Act to help finance building and improvements.

20 Aug.	United States joins I.L.O.	
24 Aug.	First trading agreement (with Cuba) signed under Reciprocal Trade Agreements Act.	

1935	7 Jan.	Panama Refining Company *et al. v.* Ryan *et al.* Case invalidates oil-production control provisions of N.R.A.
	6 May	W.P.A. set up with appropriation of $5 billion under Emergency Relief Appropriation Act of 8 April, with Harry Hopkins as Administrator.
	22 May	Soldiers Bonus Bill vetoed by President.
	27 May	Schechter Case (Schechter Poultry Corporation *v.* United States). N.R.A. subsequently disbanded.
	26 June	N.Y.A. set up as a division of W.P.A.
	5 July	Wagner Act (Wagner–Connery Act, or National Labor Relations Act) sets up N.L.R.B.
	26 July	Writers', Art and Music projects started under W.P.A.
	9 Aug.	Inter-state buses and trucks placed under I.C.C. by Motor Carrier Act.
	14 Aug.	Federal unemployment and insurance started by Social Security Act.
	26 Aug.	First convention (in Detroit) of U.A.W.
	30 Aug.	Revenue Act imposes inheritance and gift taxes, surtax, and corporation income-tax.
	8 Sept.	Huey Long assassinated (died 10 September).
	9 Nov.	Committee for Industrial Organization founded, with John L. Lewis as president.

1936	6 Jan.	United States *v.* Butler case invalidates A.A.A.
	29 Feb.	Soil Conservation and Domestic Allotment Act.
	1 June	Morehead *v.* New York case invalidates New York State Minimum Wage Law for women.
	3 Nov.	Roosevelt re-elected President (27.8 million votes); Alf Landon (Rep.) 16.7 million votes.
	30 Dec.	Sit-down strike by U.A.W. begins at G.M. plant at Flint, Michigan.

1937	20 Jan.	Inauguration of F. D. ROOSEVELT for second term. V.-P. J. N. Garner. Cabinet includes: Henry

Morgenthau Jr (Treasury), Harold Ickes (Interior), Henry A. Wallace (Agriculture), Frances Perkins (Labor).

5 Feb.　President's message to Congress recommends appointment of 'additional judges in all Federal Courts . . . where there are incumbent judges of retirement age who do not choose to retire or resign'.

11 Feb.　End of G.M. sit-down strike at Flint. U.A.W. recognised by G.M.

2 Mar.　U.S. Steel Corporation recognises unionisation of employees under Steel Workers 'Organizing Committee' (C.I.O.).

29 Mar.　West Coast Hotel *v*. Parrish Case upholds minimum wage legislation in California.

12 Apr.　N.L.R.A. upheld by Supreme Court.

24 May　Social Security Act upheld by three Supreme Court cases.

2 June　Retirement of Van Devanter from Supreme Court.

14 July　President abandons Supreme Court packing plan.

22 July　F.S.A. set up by Bankhead–Jones Farm Tenant Act, to make long-term loans for farm-purchasing.

1 Sept.　U.S.H.A. set up by Wagner–Steagall Act to provide financial assistance to states for house building.

1938　16 Feb.　Second A.A.A.

17 May　Naval Construction Act starts billion-dollar expansion.

27 May　Revenue Act reduces corporation profit-tax.

21 June　Emergency Relief Appropriation Act.

23 June　C.A.A. created to regulate air traffic.

28 June　Fair Labor Standards (Wages and Hours) Act.

30 June　(Munich Agreement signed by Hitler, Mussolini, Chamberlain, Daladier.)

18 Nov.　Congress of Industrial Organizations, created out of old Committee for Industrial Organization, elects John L. Lewis president.

1939　30 Jan.　T.V.A. upheld by Supreme Court.

14 Mar.	(Czechoslovakia invaded by Germany.)
7 Apr.	(Albania invaded by Italy.)
30 Apr.	First public television broadcast, from Empire State Building.
1 July	Federal Security Agency consolidates federal welfare agencies.
1 Sept.	(Poland invaded by Germany.)
3 Sept.	(Britain and France declare war on Germany.)

1940	3 Jan.	Roosevelt submits $8.4 billion budget, with $1.8 billion for national defence.
	19 July	Roosevelt renominated for presidency, and
	5 Nov.	Roosevelt re-elected President (27.2 million votes); Wendell Willkie (Rep.) 22.3 million votes.

The Alphabetical Agencies and other abbreviations

A.A.A.   Agricultural Adjustment Administration, set up within the Department of Agriculture, by the Agricultural Adjustment Act, 12 May 1933.

A.F. of L.   American Federation of Labor, founded by Samuel Gompers in 1886. A federation of trade unions of skilled workers.

C.A.A.   Civil Aeronautics Authority, created to regulate all air traffic, 23 June 1938.

C.C.C.   Civilian Conservation Corps, set up by the Unemployment Relief Act (Forestation), 31 March 1933. Provided work for unemployed youths, in work camps under army officers, mainly in forestry. Employed about 2 million persons 1933–42 when absorbed into Federal Works Agency. (The initials C.C.C. are occasionally used by some authors to refer to the Commodity Credit Corporation.)

C.I.O.   Congress of Industrial Organizations, set up November 1938, re-organising the former Committee for Industrial Organization of 9 November 1935 (formed out of 8 industrial unions within the A.F. of L.). John L. Lewis the moving spirit.

C.W.A.   Civil Works Administration, set up by presidential order 9 November 1933, to provide emergency unemployment relief; Harry Hopkins, Administrator. Found temporary work for 4 million on federal, state and local make-work projects. Absorbed in 1934 into F.E.R.A.

F.C.A.   Farm Credit Administration; set up 16 June 1933, to consolidate all rural credit agencies.

F.C.C.   Federal Communications Commission, set up 19 June 1934, to supervise all communications industries.

F.D.I.C.	Federal Deposit Insurance Corporation, set up by the Glass–Steagall Banking Reform Act of June 1933. Gave federal guarantee to all bank deposits up to $2500, a figure subsequently raised several times.
F.E.R.A.	Federal Emergency Relief Administration, set up by the Federal Emergency Relief Act 12 May 1933.
F.F.B.	Federal Farm Board, set up by the Agricultural Marketing Act of 15 June 1929 to make loans to stabilisation corporations.
F.F.M.C.	Federal Farm Mortgage Corporation, set up by the Farm Mortgage Refinancing Act of 1934, to operate under the F.C.A. for provision of further aid to farmers.
F.H.A.	Federal Housing Authority, set up by the National Housing Act of 28 June 1934, to stimulate residential construction through federal mortgages.
F.L.S.A.	Fair Labor Standards (Wages and Hours) Act, 25 June 1938, providing 40-hour week (went into effect 24 October 1940).
F.S.A. (i)	Farm Security Administration, set up 22 July 1937, to make long-term loans for farm purchase.
F.S.A. (ii)	Federal Security Agency, set up 1 July 1939, to consolidate federal welfare agencies.
F.T.C.	Federal Trade Commission, set up by the Clayton Act of 1914, to supervise enforcement of anti-monopoly policy.
G.M.	General Motors. Founded 1908, developed into vast manufacturing empire, especially under presidency of Alfred P. Sloan, 1923–37.
H.O.L.C.	Home Owners' Loan Corporation, set up 13 June 1933, to re-finance home mortgages.
I.C.C.	Interstate Commerce Commission, set up by the Interstate Commerce Act of 4th February 1887, intended to bring under federal regulation all railroads engaged in inter-state commerce.
I.L.O.	International Labor Organisation, joined by the U.S.A. 20 August 1934.
I.W.W.	Industrial (*not* International) Workers of the World, founded 1905. A revolutionary labour union, led by Eugene V. Debs. Sank into oblivion during First World War.

K.K.K.	Ku Klux Klan, a secret society revived in Georgia in 1915, hostile to minority and non-conformist groups. Spread in South and Mid-west in 1920s, at one time claiming membership of 4 million.
N.I.R.A.	National Industrial Recovery Act, 16 June 1933, setting up N.R.A. and P.W.A.
N.L.B.	National Labor Board, set up under the N.R.A. to enforce collective bargaining, 5 August 1933; chairman, Senator Robert F. Wagner.
N.L.R.B.	National Labor Relations Board, set up by the National Labor Relations Act (the Wagner–Connery Act) of 5 July 1935. Aimed at prevention and remedy of unfair labour practices.
N.R.A.	National Recovery Administration, set up under the N.I.R.A., 16 June 1933; Administrator, General Hugh S. Johnson.
N.Y.A.	National Youth Administration, set up as a division of W.P.A., 26 June 1935.
P.W.A.	Public Works Administration, set up under N.I.R.A., 16 June 1933; Administrator, Harold L. Ickes (Secretary of the Interior).
R.F.C.	Reconstruction Finance Corporation, set up by Congress, 22 January 1932, under Hoover's presidency, mainly to assist banks through loans.
S.E.C.	Securities and Exchange Commission, set up 6 June 1934. An independent agency of 5 members to supervise activities on the stock markets and enforce the Federal Securities Act of 1933 and the Securities Exchange Act of 1934.
T.V.A.	Tennessee Valley Authority, set up by the Tennessee Valley Authority Act, 18 May 1933.
U.A.W.	United Automobile Workers, union chartered by the A.F. of L., 1935.
U.S.H.A.	United States Housing Authority, set up 1 September 1937 to remedy housing shortage by providing financial assistance to the states.
W.P.A.	Works Progress Administration, set up 8 April 1935 under the Emergency Relief Appropriation Act, with funds of $5 billion for 'work relief and to increase

employment by providing useful projects'. Main emphasis was on job creation.

Butler Case (United States *v.* Butler *et al.*), 6 January 1936. By 6 votes to 3, the Supreme Court held the imposition of a tax on the food-processing industry to finance payments to farmers who agreed to crop restrictions to be 'the expropriation of money from one group for the benefit of another' and therefore not a legitimate use of taxing power. This had the effect of pronouncing as unconstitutional the first A.A.A.

Fordney–McCumber Tariff, 19 September 1922.

The Underwood Tariff of 1913 had made first significant tariff reduction since Civil War. After the First World War Fordney–McCumber raised tariffs to the highest level ever.

Hawley–Smoot Tariff, 19 June 1930.

This increased tariffs still further, to give more protection to U.S. industry after the onset of depression, and established the Tariff Commission.

Norris–La Guardia Anti-Injunction Act, 23 March 1932.

First important piece of congressional legislation in support of labour unions. Restricted use of injunction in labour disputes and made 'yellow-dog' contracts non-enforceable at law. Defined 'labor dispute' widely enough to increase scope of trade union activities.

Sacco–Vanzetti Trial, May 1920.

Nicola Sacco and Bartolomeo Vanzetti, Italian immigrants and admitted anarchists, were accused of a murder committed in April 1920, convicted on flimsy evidence, and executed on 23 August 1927. The case aroused great international as well as domestic concern, since many believed they were convicted because of their origins, class and political beliefs.

Scopes Trial, July 1925. 'The Monkey Trial.'

Trial at Dayton, Tennessee, of a high-school teacher, John T. Scopes, for teaching Darwin's theory of evolution. Prosecution led by William Jennings Bryan; Scopes defended by Clarence Darrow. Scopes fined $100. Trial dramatised in play *Inherit the Wind*.

Schechter Case (Schechter Poultry Assoc. *v.* U.S.), or the 'Sick chicken case', 27 May 1935. Supreme Court unanimously decided that the N.I.R.A. involved an unconstitutional delegation of legislative powers by Congress to the President.

Teapot Dome scandal.

In 1915 President Wilson proclaimed an area of over 9000 acres in Wyoming to be a petroleum reserve for the U.S. Navy. In April 1922 the Teapot Dome was leased by Harding's Secretary of the Interior, A. B. Fall, to oil magnate Harry F. Sinclair. After congressional and other enquiries the transfer was declared invalid by the Supreme Court in 1927.

Volstead Act (Prohibition Enforcement Act).

Passed by Congress over President Wilson's veto, 28 October 1919, going into effect January 1920. Prohibited sale and consumption of intoxicating beverages, defined as those containing over one-half of 1 per cent alcohol. Repealed 1933.

Wagner–Connery Act.

After the Schechter Case, the labour clauses of the N.I.R.A. were re-enacted as the National Labor Relations Act, 5 July 1935, creating the N.L.R.B. Gave American trade unions clear legal status and facilitated their rapid growth after 1935.

References

I<small>NTRODUCTION</small>

1. H. L. Mencken, cited in W. E. Leuchtenburg, *The Perils of Prosperity, 1914–32* (1958) p. 7.

1 F<small>ROM</small> T<small>ANKS AND</small> T<small>ORPEDOES TO</small> T<small>RACTORS AND</small> T<small>IN</small> L<small>IZZIES</small> 1918–21

1. A. D. H. Kaplan, *Big Enterprise in a Competitive System* (1964) *passim*.

2 C<small>OMMON</small> F<small>EATURES OF THE</small> I<small>NTER-WAR</small> Y<small>EARS</small>

1. For further discussion, see Richard A. Easterlin, *Population, Labor Force and Long Swings in Economic Growth* (1968).

3 P<small>ROSPERITY</small> 1922–9

1. André Siegfried, *America Comes of Age* (1927) p. 35.
2. Paul H. Douglas, *Real Wages in the United States, 1890–1926* (1930).
3. Irving Bernstein, *The Lean Years: A History of the American Worker 1920–1933* (1960) p. 65.
4. Siegfried, *America Comes of Age* (1927). Juxtaposition of passages from ch. XI, 'Labour and the Standard of Living' and ch. XXVII, 'European *vs* American Civilization'.
5. Charles N. Glaab, 'Metropolis and Suburb: The Changing American City', in *Change and Continuity in Twentieth Century America: the 1920s*, ed. J. Braeman *et al.* (1968).
6. Bernard Fay, cited in Glaab, *ibid.*
7. Walter Lippmann, *The Atlantic Monthly*, 139 (Feb. 1927), cited in *Politics of the Nineteen Twenties*, ed. G. L. Shover (1970).
8. The problems are analysed in M. Leven and K. R. Wright, *The Income Structure of the United States* (Brookings Institution, 1938).
9. For a more pessimistic view, see Bernstein, *The Lean Years*. The figures quoted in the text are from *Historical Statistics of the United States* (U.S. Bureau of the Census, 1960).

10. See Bernstein, *The Lean Years*, pp. 66 ff.
11. M. Leven, H. G. Moulton and C. Warburton, *America's Capacity to Consume* (Brookings Institution, 1934) p. 158.
12. *Ibid.* pp. 103–4. Estimates based on income-tax returns.
13. See Albert V. Romasco, *The Poverty of Abundance: Hoover, the Nation and The Depression* (1965).
14. Bernstein, *The Lean Years*, p. 59.
15. For further analysis, see in particular Alfred D. Chandler, *Strategy and Structure* (1962).
16. E.g. F. L. Allen, *Only Yesterday* (1931); J. K. Galbraith, *The Great Crash 1929* (1955).
17. Malcolm Falkus, 'U.S. Economic Policy and the "Dollar Gap" of the 1920s', *Economic History Review* (Nov. 1971).
18. E. R. Wicker, 'Federal Reserve Monetary Policy 1922–33: A Reinterpretation', *Journal of Political Economy* (1965), and *Federal Reserve Monetary Policy, 1917–1933* (1966).
19. For a contemporary analysis of the problems of agriculture and the shortcomings of the proposals, see Rexford Tugwell, 'Reflections on Farm Relief', *Political Science Quarterly* (Dec. 1928), reprinted in *Politics of the Nineteen Twenties*, ed. Shover.

4 DEPRESSION 1929–33

1. On Hoover and the business community, see Romasco, *The Poverty of Abundance*. In writing this section I have also had access to an unpublished manuscript 'Herbert Hoover and the Business Community 1929–1932' by Dr Susan H. Armitage, now at the University of Colorado.
2. Herbert Hoover, *Memoirs*, vol. III, *The Great Depression 1929–1941* (1952) p. 420.
3. This aspect of the period is examined in detail in Jordan A. Schwarz, *The Interregnum of Despair* (1970).
4. Anne O'Hare McCormick, 7 May 1933, cited in Frank Freidel, *The New Deal and the American People* (1964) pp. 4–5.
5. For a more detailed discussion see, for example, M. W. Lee, *Macroeconomics: Fluctuations, Growth and Stability*, 3rd edn (1963).
6. Cited in Frank Freidel, *Franklin D. Roosevelt*, vol. III (1954) p. 354.

6 THE NEW DEAL: SUCCESS OR FAILURE?

1. From G. VON Haberler, *Prosperity and Depression* 4th edn (1958).

2. E. Cary Brown, 'Fiscal policy in the Thirties: a Reappraisal', *American Economic Review*, XLVI (1956).

3. Corwin Edwards, 'Thurman Arnold and the Antitrust Laws', *Political Science Quarterly*, LVIII (1943).

4. D. Wecter, *The Age of the Great Depression* (1971) p. 176.

5. E. Lundberg, *Business Cycles and Economic Policy* (1957)

Further Reading

GENERAL

ADAMS, D. K., *America in the Twentieth Century* (1967).

ARNDT, H. W., *The Economic Lessons of the Nineteen-Thirties* (1944).

CHANDLER, A. D., *Strategy and Structure: Chapters in the History of American Industrial Enterprise* (1962).

COCHRAN, T. C., *The American Business System: a Historical Perspective 1900–1955* (1957).

DOUGLAS, P. H., *Real Wages in the United States, 1890–1926* (1930).

EASTERLIN, R. A., *Population, Labor Force and Long Swings in Economic Growth* (1968).

FRIEDMAN, M. and SCHWARTZ, A. J., *A Monetary History of the United States 1867–1960* (1963).

HABERLER, G. VON, *Prosperity and Depression*, 4th edn (1958).

HOGAN, J. D. and IANNI, F. A. J., *American Social Legislation* (1956).

JOSEPHSON, M. and H., *Al Smith, Hero of the Cities* (1969).

KAPLAN, A. D. H., *Big Enterprise in a Competitive System* (1964).

LEE, M. W., *Macroeconomics: Fluctuations, Growth and Stability*, 3rd edn (1963).

LEVEN, M., and WRIGHT K. R., *The Income Structure of the United States* (Brookings Institution, 1938).

LYND, R. S. and H. M., *Middletown* (1929).

McCOY, D. R., *Calvin Coolidge: the Quiet President* (1967).

ROBERTSON, R. M., *History of the American Economy*, 3rd edn. (1973).

SINCLAIR, A., *The Available Man: The Life Behind the Masks of Warren Gamaliel Harding* (1965).

WICKER, E. R., *Federal Reserve Monetary Policy, 1917–1933* (1966).

THE 1920S

ALLEN, F. L., *Only Yesterday* (1931).

BERNSTEIN, I., *The Lean Years: a History of the American Worker, 1920–1933* (1960).

BRAEMAN, J. et al., *Change and Continuity in Twentieth Century America: the 1920s* (1968).

BUTLER, H. B., *Industrial Relations in the United States* (I.L.O., 1927).

CARTER, P. A., *The Twenties in America* (1968).

GALBRAITH, J. K., *The Great Crash, 1929* (1955).

HICKS, J. D., *Republican Ascendancy, 1921–1933* (1960).

LEUCHTENBURG, W. E., *The Perils of Prosperity, 1914–32* (1958).

LEVEN, M., MOULTON, H. G. and WARBURTON, C., *America's Capacity to Consume* (Brookings Institution, 1934).

SHOVER, J. L., *Politics of the Nineteen Twenties* (1970).

SIEGFRIED, A., *America Comes of Age: a French Analysis* (1927).

SINCLAIR, A., *Prohibition : the Era of Excess* (1962).

SOULE, G. H., *Prosperity Decade* (1947).

VATTER, H. G., 'Has there been a Twentieth-Century Consumer Durables Revolution?', *The Journal of Economic History*, XXVII (March 1967).

HOOVER AND HIS YEARS

ALLEN, F. L., *Since Yesterday* (1940).

CHANDLER, L. V., *America's Greatest Depression, 1929–1941* (1970).

FRIEDMAN, M., and SCHWARTZ, A. J., *The Great Contraction 1929–1933* (1964).

LEIGHTON, I., *The Aspirin Age* (1940).

ROMASCO, A. U., *The Poverty of Abundance: Hoover, the Nation, the Depression* (1965).

SCHWARZ, J. A., *The Interregnum of Despair: Hoover, Congress and the Depression* (1970).

WARREN, H. G., *Herbert Hoover and the Great Depression* (1959).

WECTER, D., *The Age of the Great Depression, 1929–1941* (1948).

ROOSEVELT AND HIS YEARS

AMHERST COLLEGE (eds), *Problems in American Civilization: the New Deal* (1949).

BLUM, J. M., *From the Diaries of Henry Morgenthau: Years of Crisis*, vol. I, *1928–1938* (1959).

BROWN, E. C., 'Fiscal Policy in the Thirties: a Reappraisal', *American Economic Review*, XLVI (Dec. 1956).

BURNS, J. MacGregor, *Roosevelt: the Lion and the Fox* (1956).

CHANDLER, L. V., *America's Greatest Depression, 1929–1941* (1970).

CONKIN, P. K., *The New Deal* (1967).

DERBER, M. and YOUNG, E. (eds.), *Labor and the New Deal* (1957).

FREIDEL, F. B., *Franklin D. Roosevelt*, vol. 3, *The Triumph* (1956).

FREIDEL, F. B. (ed.), *The New Deal and the American People* (1964).

JOHNSON, H. S., *The Blue Eagle from Egg to Earth* (1935).

LEUCHTENBURG, W. E., *Franklin D. Roosevelt and the New Deal: 1932–1940* (1963).

MAJOR, J. S. H., *The New Deal* (1967).

McCOY, D. R., *Coming of Age* (1973).

MITCHELL, B., *Depression Decade, 1929–1941* (1947).

MOLEY, R., *After Seven Years* (1939).

MOLEY, R., *The First New Deal* (1966).

NOURSE, E. G. et al., *Three Years of the A.A.A.* (1937).

PERKINS, Frances, *The Roosevelt I Knew* (1947).

SCHLESINGER JR, A. M., *The Age of Roosevelt*: vol. 1, *The Crisis of the Old Order* (1957); vol. 2, *The Coming of the New Deal* (1959); vol. 3, *The Politics of Upheaval* (1960).

WECTER, D., *The Age of the Great Depression, 1929–1941* (1948).

WOLTERS, R., *Negroes and the Great Depression* (1970).

Subject Index

181

Name Index